NutriBullet

RECIPE BOOK

Savoury Soups

71 Delicious, Healthy, Exquisite Soups & Sauces for your NutriBullet

Diana Clayton

DISCLAIMER

This book is written to supplement the NutriBullet Nutrition Extractor and has no affiliation with NutriBullet LLC. NutriBullet LLC was not involved in the recipe creation or development of this book.

Every effort has been made to ensure that the information in this book is accurate and complete, however, the author and the publisher do not warrant the accuracy of the information, text and graphics contained within the book due to the rapidly changing nature of science and research. The author and the publisher do not hold any responsibility for errors, omissions or contrary interpretation of the subject matter herein.

NutriBullet

RECIPE BOOK

Savoury Soups

CONTENTS

THICK AND CREAMY SOUPS 33

SUPER SMOOTH SOUPS 43

WARMING BROTHS 59

SAUCES 69

DIPS AND DRESSINGS 87

Conclusion   95

Recommendations   96

INTRODUCTION

Chances are that if you already own a Nutribullet then you are familiar with the concept of a Nutriblast; essentially a nutritionally powerful smoothie that contains all of the fibre and the under-skin goodness of fresh produce but without the off putting fibrous quality.

But what if your Nutribullet became just another extension of your everyday cooking tools and could be used to boost the nutrient content of *many* of your daily meals?

Well, your NutriBullet *can* become another extension of your everyday cooking tools and Diana is here to show you how. A wonderful place to start is with soups, sauces, and dips! With a little creative thinking your Nutribullet can be used to create flavour and nutrient combinations that can then be added to other ingredients and heated as part of a filling soup or tasty sauce for pasta; all with far greater nutritional value than their original recipe counterparts.

Most who have purchased the Nutribullet have done so because they understand the nutritional benefits of raw ingredients and that conventional juicing discards much of the beneficial fibre and phytochemicals within the plants; not to mention the time and the mess.

Likewise, most of the ingredients in this book have been chosen with their nutritional scope in mind.

Are you ready to get the most from your Nutribullet? Wonderful! Then let's move on.

The Nutribullet Kitchen

THE BEST OF BOTH WORLDS

Nutritionally speaking, many vitamins, minerals, and accessory nutrients such as phytochemicals, are most abundant in raw plant foods. It is also a well-known fact that minerals in foods become far more readily available to the body when they are physically broken down. The Nutribullet of course breaks them down much further than most tools on the market, thereby enhancing nutrient availability as well as fl avour and texture.

On the other hand though, we eat food for reasons that go beyond nutrient value. Aside from the many wonderful fl avours that come from fresh vibrant raw fruit and vegetables, cooking is one of the ways to intro-duce depth and variety into our meals. Consider the diff erence between the sharp, acrid fl avour of raw onion and the sweet silky depths of that same onion when slowly cooked to melting perfection. Put the two together on the same plate and the contrast of elements brings them together as one glorious whole.

In the same context as the onion example above taking the techniques of cooking, with all of the relevant benefi ts that they bring, and putting them together with the diff erent fl avours, textures (and of course nutrient value) of blended raw produce really does provide you with the best of both worlds and greater scope in the kitchen.

The extensive recipe section that forms the focus of this guide not only provides you with delicious ideas but takes you through the essential processes required to make perfect soups and sauces.

Each recipe comes with nutritional data for the fi nished dish, as well as a description of the key nutrients and health benefi ts of the focal ingre - dients. Tips and tricks are given throughout as well as clear concise methods that are easy to follow; our aim is to provide you with all the knowledge and confi dence that you need to prepare a healthy range of soups dips, and sauces for you and your family to enjoy.

Happy eating!

Diana

STOCKS

Some of the soup recipes that follow call for the use of stock. So if you need a few great stock recipes to utilize, then this is for you.

The idea of making and using stocks makes most home cooks shrink away in horror at the thought of boiling big pans of bones for hours on end; a process for which life is just too short. However, there is no need to fear as stocks are actually pretty simple and a great way of using up kitchen waste as well as wringing every scrap of nutrition from your hard earned ingredients.

Many soups do not need stock, some centre around a decent stock, yet all will benefitf rom the round savoury depth that stock brings. There are as many types of stock as there are soup but here we give you recipes for the main four; of which chicken is the most versatile. After that, having a good fishstockunderyourbeltis essential for those fragrant seafood broth type dishes that taste so good on holiday.

If any of our soup recipes really need to be made with stock then it will be mentioned in the ingredients list; other than that use water or the prescribed liquid. Bear in mind that if you have chicken stock always at han,d there is not a soup in the world that won't taste better for it.

Chicken Stock

The stock that you will find most useful, and that delivers the best neutral flavour, is chicken stock. Unless you are a really keen cook in the habit of deboning your own poultry it is most likely that you will be dealing with cooked leftover chicken carcasses. These make excellent stock, with a good depth of flavour, and do not need to be cooked as long as raw bones. It is a good idea to chop the bones up, paying special attention to the long bones of the legs and wings, as this releases nutrients and flavour from within the bones. We like a good chickeny base to work with, with no other flavours at all, so use only bones and water for chicken stock. You can tell good quality chicken by the stock it makes; a battery farmed chicken will not make a good jelly and it may even taste slightly fishy because of the unnatural feed. You will get the best results if you give the stock the full two hours but as the bones are not raw it is safe to give it less time if needs dictate.

SERVINGS: 4
PREPARATION TIME: 15 minutes
COOKING TIME: 2 hours

INGREDIENTS

1 chicken carcass, chopped, no skin

2 litres water, less for shorter cooking time

1. Put the chopped bones in a deep saucepan with the water.

2. Bring to the boil, skimming any scum that appears on the surface, and turn down to a gentle simmer. If you are in a hurry, please be aware that a higher heat will not speed up the process, it will actually result in cloudy bitter stock. You need somewhere between a slow bubbling boil and a gentle shimmer.

3. Your stock is ready when reduced by half.

4. Strain immediately (never leave stock ingredients in the stock to cool) and leave to cool.

Fish Stock

After vegetable stock, fish is the quickest but also the most feared. There are very few instances, especially in this guide, when you want a fish stock as it can be quite pervasive. That said, a great fish broth or stew will need a good stock to get that magnificent depth of flavour. An overcooked fish stock will be bitter and cloudy so do not make the mistake of leaving it for a long time.

SERVINGS: 4
PREPARATION TIME: 10 minutes
COOKING TIME: 30 minutes

INGREDIENTS

500 g raw fish trimmings, but not entrails
2 stalks parsley
1 onion, skin on, chopped in half
1 stick celery, chopped in half
1 carrot, chopped in half
1 litre water
4 black peppercorns

1. Place all of the ingredients in a saucepan and cover with the cold water.
2. Bring up to the boil, turn the heat down and simmer for 30 minutes. You will need to skim any scum that forms on the surface; it is simply protein particles from the fish.
3. Strain immediately and cool.

Meat Stock

|||||||||||||||||||||||||||||||||||||||||||||||||||||||||||||||||||||||||||||||||||||||||||

When talking meat stock, the best way to go is beef. Lamb stock can be somewhat overpowering and greasy, whilst pork stock is not used so much in everyday soup making and sauce cookery. You could ask your butcher for raw bones or use the leftover bones from a bone-in roast. Marrow bones make an excellent stock. A good beef broth is going to take several hours; about 4 to be exact, longer if possible.

SERVINGS: 4
PREPARATION TIME: 10 minutes
COOKING TIME: 4 hours

INGREDIENTS

1 kg marrow bones
500 g beef shin
2 onions, skin on, halved
2 sticks celery, halved
1 tbsp. black peppercorns

1. Put the chopped bones in a deep saucepan with the water.

2. Bring to the boil, skimming any scum that appears on the surface, and turn down to a gentle simmer. If you are in a hurry, please be aware that a higher heat will not speed up the process, it will actually result in cloudy bitter stock. You need somewhere between a slow bubbling boil and a gentle shimmer.

3. Your stock is ready when reduced by half.

4. Strain immediately (never leave stock ingredients in the stock to cool) and leave to cool.

Vegetable Stock

Of all the stocks, vegetable is the quickest to make. A stock is there solely to enhance soup and the flavours within must never dominate. To that end, a stock is never salted. Make your vegetable stocks from all of your vegetable trimmings and unwanted herb stalks. Think about what you are putting in; unless for a specific purpose you may want to avoid fennel, for instance. You can make a vegetable stock with more depth by cooking the vegetable trimmings in stock first; in much the same manner as making a soup. This recipe is a simple guide, using the browning in fat method as it is the quickest route to a flavoursome stock; we keep the flavours neutral rather than adding extra herbs.

SERVINGS: 4
PREPARATION TIME: 10 minutes
COOKING TIME: 15 minutes

INGREDIENTS

1 tbsp. butter or oil
1 onion, chopped
1 carrot, chopped
1 stick celery, chopped
Vegetable and herb
   trimmings
1 litre water

1. In a large deep saucepan heat the oil and add the rest of the ingredients. Cook over a low heat until the vegetables begin to cook down (a process known as sweating).

2. Now add the water, bring it to a gentle boil, and simmer for 15 minutes; keep the pan partially covered with a lid.

3. Strain the stock and leave to cool.

COOLING SOUPS

There are not many vegetables that respond well to being souped when raw and even fewer that are delicious when cold. This short section presents a few failsafe chilled soups that will please the most ardent of critics.

The countries that have chilled or cold soups amongst their repertoire are usually the ones that burn brightly under a hot sun and whose people are in need of rehydration. As well as cooling in them-selves, they often contain ingredients that can improve hydration, such as cucumber, or encourage sweating, such as chillies.

None of these soups require cooking so present no more diffi-culty on a hot day than a smoothie or lemonade. The fact that these are savoury, and therefore require a pinch of salt, means that you are replacing valuable electrolytes that can be lost in the heat.

Cucumber, Yoghurt, and Pistachio

A cooling cucumber soup, this one with the addition of creamy yoghurt. Great for soothing the stomach and the soul, this soup is also excellent for curing the ills of the morning after the night before. Don't be shy with the garlic and don't be tempted to omit the salt. Garnish with pistachio nuts for added interest.

SERVINGS: 1
PREPARATION TIME: 15 minutes
TOTAL TIME: 15 minutes

INGREDIENTS

½ cucumber, chopped
4 tbsp. fresh mint
1 pinch sea salt
1 clove garlic
100 grams yoghurt
150 ml water
2 tbsp. chopped pistachios

1. Blend of the ingredients together, apart from the nuts, in the large cup with the extractor blade.

2. Garnish with the pistachio nuts for a beautiful contrast of colour.

NUTRITIONAL VALUES PER SERVING: 177 calories, 7.6g total fat, 5mg cholesterol, 328.2mg sodium, 569.7mg potassium, 15.2g carbohydrates, 2.9g fibre, 7g sugar, 14.7g protein

Green Herb Gazpacho

Not many ingredients actually lend themselves well to cold, or indeed raw, soup. Luckily cucumber is not one of them, which explains why it crops up so often. Not only is the texture perfect but the cooling quality of cucumber makes it the ideal thing for a hot day. Many cold soups need to be super chilled with the addition of ice cubes; this one included. Full of vibrant green produce this cooling soup doubles up as an excellent detoxifier and antioxidant boost.

SERVINGS: 1
PREPARATION TIME: 15 minutes
TOTAL TIME: 15 minutes

INGREDIENTS

½ celery stick, chopped
½ green pepper, chopped
½ cucumber, chopped
1 garlic clove
1 handful rocket
2 tbsp. parsley
1 tbsp. coriander
1 tbsp. mint
1 tbsp. basil
2 tbsp. breadcrumbs
1 pinch salt
freshly ground black pepper
1 tbsp. olive oil
½ tsp balsamic vinegar
100 ml water
4 ice cubes

1. Place all ingredients in the large cup and blend with the extractor blade until smooth.

2. Check the seasoning and serve.

NUTRITIONAL VALUES PER SERVING: 230 calories, 14.9g total fat, 0mg cholesterol, 425.9mg sodium, 650mg potassium, 21g carbohydrates, 4.7g fibre, 6g sugar, 4.8g protein

Mexican Avocado Soup

Another no cook soup, this one takes the flavours of guacamole and serves them as a creamy and comforting soup full of vibrancy and life. Avocado is full of wonderful nutrients and fats that are essential for health; not to mention beneficial to your skin and hair. Added sweetcorn adds textural interest and a touch of sweet flavour.

SERVINGS: 1
PREPARATION TIME: 15 minutes
TOTAL TIME: 15 minutes

INGREDIENTS

1 ripe avocado
½ red chilli, chopped
½ clove garlic, crushed
1 lime, juice only
1 tbsp. olive oil
2 tbsp. coriander leaf
50 g tinned sweetcorn

1. Add all of the ingredients to the large cup and pulse once or twice to create a blended yet textural soup. The avocado should be smooth, but the sweetcorn should be chunky and the chilli and the coriander in visible flecks. If you blend it too far then the flavours all meld into one rather than contrast with each other.

2. Serve the soup at room temperature, or chilled.

NUTRITIONAL VALUES PER SERVING: 442 calories, 40.5g total fat, 0mg cholesterol, 22.9mg sodium, 1073mg potassium, 24.9g carbohydrates, 14.3g fibre, 2.9g sugar, 4.6g protein.

Watercress and Yoghurt

A refreshing chilled soup with the peppery bite of watercress and the sharp acidity of yoghurt. Hugely nutritious with plenty of calcium for strong bones and a good dose of vitamin C to fight infection. Chopped walnuts add texture as well antioxidant vitamin E. Sooo good!

SERVINGS: 1
PREPARATION TIME: 15 minutes
TOTAL TIME: 15 minutes

INGREDIENTS

50 g watercress
100 ml low fat yoghurt
100 ml water
2 tbsp. walnuts
1 pinch salt
Freshly ground black pepper

1. Place all of the ingredients in the large cup and pulse with the extractor blade until smooth.

2. Chill before serving or reduce the amount of water and replace with ice cubes; you may want to be quite generous with the salt.

NUTRITIONAL VALUES PER SERVING: 169 calories, 11.4g total fat, 6.1mg cholesterol, 384.9mg sodium, 476.6mg potassium, 10.3g carbohydrates, 1.5g fibre, <1g sugar, 8.8g protein.

HEARTY SOUPS

These are the big chunky soups for when you need a warming meal and extra sustenance. Hearty ingredients such as starchy vegetables and pulses are cooked with robust flavours and pleasing textures that provide everything you need when the weather is cold or you feel under par.

Spiced Sweet Potato and Spinach

A thick, chunky soup with soft sweet potato and its favourite partner spinach. Curry spices add fragrant heat to turn this into a deeply satisfying meal. You can alter the chilli content to suit. The nutrients in spinach are actually more accessible when cooked so in this recipe the NutriBullet is used to make short work of the spice paste.

SERVINGS: 1
PREPARATION TIME: 15 minutes
COOKING TIME: 20 minutes

INGREDIENTS

1 tbsp. coconut oil
1 medium sweet potato, peeled and diced
50 g baby spinach leaves
250 ml water or stock

FOR THE SPICE PASTE

1 cloves garlic
25 mm ginger
1 red chillies
2 tbsp. fresh coriander, chopped
1 tsp cumin seeds
1 tsp coriander seeds
1 squeeze fresh lime juice
1 pinch sea salt

1. Boil the sweet potato in a large pan of water until tender; roughly 20 minutes.

2. Put all of the 'spice paste' ingredients in the small cup and pulse with the milling blade to a coarse paste.

3. Heat the coconut oil in a saucepan and add the sweet potato, spinach and spice paste. Fry for 2 minutes until the spices release their aromas and the spinach has wilted.

4. Pour in 250ml water, or stock, and heat to serve.

NUTRITIONAL VALUES PER SERVING: 281 calories, 14.9g total fat, 0mg cholesterol, 414.7mg sodium, 1000.2mg potassium, 36g carbohydrates, 7g fibre, 8.3g sugar, 5.4g protein.

Spinach and Lentil Dal

This fragrant dal is cooked in the pan, using the NutriBullet to make a fresh spice paste. Comfort food at its best, the soft lentils are high in fibre that keep blood sugar down and lower cholesterol. Spinach provides B vitamins and minerals such as magnesium and iron whilst the garlic and ginger have remarkable medicinal properties. Do use curry leaves if you can find them as they add a lovely savoury edge.

SERVINGS: 1
PREPARATION TIME: 10 minutes
COOKING TIME: 20 minutes

INGREDIENTS

75 g red lentils, washed
250 ml water
1 onion, roughly chopped
1 clove garlic, roughly chopped
25 mm ginger, roughly chopped
1 red chilli, roughly chopped
1 tsp cumin seeds
1 tbsp. coconut oil
1 tsp mustard seeds
1 tsp curry leaves
1 tsp turmeric
1 pinch salt
50 g spinach
½ lemon, juice only
2 tbsp. coriander, chopped

1. Cook the lentils in the water over a medium heat until soft. Set aside without draining.

2. Put the onion, garlic, ginger, chilli and cumin in the small cup with a squeeze of lemon. Pulse until you have a coarse paste.

3. Heat the oil in a large saucepan and add the mustard seeds and the curry leaves (if using). When the seeds start to sizzle and pop, add the paste with the turmeric and a pinch of salt. Stir for 2 minutes.

4. Add the spinach and stir until it wilts. Then pour in the lentils with their cooking water.

5. Heat to serve and garnish with a squeeze of lemon juice and fresh coriander leaf

NUTRITIONAL VALUES PER SERVING: 343 calories, 16.5g total fat, 0mg cholesterol, 364.9mg sodium, 1310mg potassium, 43.3g carbohydrates, 12.8g fibre, 11.3g sugar, 13g protein.

Spinach, Pepper, and Chickpeas

A chunky stew like soup that is best made with fresh chicken stock. Instead of fragrant spices, the soup is enhanced with some good quality paprika, oil and lemon juice, then topped off with a little feta cheese for a sharp yet creamy contrast. The spinach is blended in the NutriBullet to form a rich green base for the soup and retain maximum freshness.

SERVINGS: 1
PREPARATION TIME: 10 minutes
COOKING TIME: 20 minutes

INGREDIENTS

1 tbsp. olive oil
½ red pepper, thinly sliced
1 pinch salt
½ onion, thinly sliced
1 tbsp. paprika
1 clove garlic, crushed
1 tomato, chopped
1/3 tin chickpeas, drained
75 ml chicken stock
    or water
50 g spinach
Freshly ground black pepper
2 tbsp. fresh parsley,
    chopped
1 squeeze lemon juice
25 g feta cheese

1. Heat the oil in a saucepan and add the peppers with a pinch of salt. After 5 minutes, when the peppers have started to soften, add the onions.

2. Continue to cook the onions and peppers for about 15 minutes until they are soft and golden, Add the garlic, paprika and tomato then cook for another minute.

3. Add the chickpeas and leave over a gentle heat whilst you do the spinach.

4. Put the spinach with the stock into the large cup and pulse with the extractor blade until pureed. Add to the pan and stir to heat through.

5. Check your seasoning and serve the hot soup with a squeeze of lemon, chopped fresh parsley and crumbled feta cheese.

NUTRITIONAL VALUES PER SERVING: 395 calories, 23g total fat, 24.5mg cholesterol, 960 mg sodium, 1277mg potassium, 37.7g carbohydrates, 11.7g fibre, 12.6g sugar, 14.g protein.

White Beans with Onion and Tomato

Full of fibre, beans help to lower blood sugar and reduce cholesterol. Onions contain a variety of compounds beneficial in the fight against modern disease and have powerful anti-cancer and blood sugar lowering properties. Antioxidant lycopene is more readily available in cooked tomatoes than in raw and oil improves absorption even further. Enjoy a rich and flavourful bowl of warming beans on a cold day, rich with olive oil, sweet tomatoes and the fresh flavour of flat leaf parsley.

SERVINGS: 1
PREPARATION TIME: 10 minutes
COOKING TIME: 15 minutes

INGREDIENTS

1 tbsp. olive oil
1 onion, chopped
1 pinch salt
20 ripe cherry tomatoes
1 clove garlic
½ tin cannellini beans
2 tbsp. fresh parsley
Olive oil for drizzle

1. Heat the oil in a frying pan and add the onions with a pinch of salt. Fry for 2 minutes until softening and beginning to brown.

2. Add the tomatoes and keep cooking over a medium heat for a further 10 minutes. The tomatoes should soften and collapse yet brown on the skin side. Add the garlic and stir for a minute more.

3. Add the beans with a squeeze of lemon juice. Check the seasoning and remove from the heat

4. When the mix has cooled a little, put half into the large cup with 100ml water. Pulse until broken down yet still coarse; add more liquid if necessary.

5. Return the blended mixture to the pan and heat through.

6. Serve hot with a drizzle of oil and fresh parsley. Garnish with a little chopped raw onion and tomato if desired.

NUTRITIONAL VALUES PER SERVING: 623 calories, 20.1g total fat, 0mg cholesterol, 347.5mg sodium, 2800.6mg potassium, 89.4g carbohydrates, 21.3g fibre, 5.3g sugar, 28.2g protein.

LIGHTER SOUPS

These soups are all blended soups, but unlike those in the super smooth or thick and creamy sections, their ingredients dictate a lighter less creamy feel; depending on how you feel about chilled soups they may well suit being served cold as well as providing a light lunch or starter on blustery days.

Charred Pepper, Parsley, and Pine Nut Soup

Here we make the most of the wonderful sweet taste and silky texture of peppers to make a light soup. When it comes to lycopene, a great phytochemical, we tend to think tomato, but red peppers contain just as much lycopene as tomatoes do. They are also an excellent source of vitamin C. Instead of roasting the peppers, which in a conventional oven often lacks the charred exterior, we are going to fry the sliced peppers over a high heat, skins left on. Simply pureed with parsley, toasted pine nuts and a little olive oil, this is a deceptively easy yet elegant soup.

SERVINGS: 1
PREPARATION TIME: 10 minutes
COOKING TIME: 15 minutes

INGREDIENTS

2 tbsp. pine nuts
1 tbsp. olive oil
1 large red pepper, skin left on, deseeded and sliced.
1 pinch salt
200 ml stock or water
4 tbsp. parsley
Freshly ground black pepper

1. First, toast the pine nuts for a minute in a dry frying pan.
2. Remove the pine nuts from the pan and add half of the oil and the peppers with a pinch of salt.
3. Fry over a medium high heat so that the skins char slightly and the peppers go soft; about 10 minutes.
4. Place the peppers, and the rest of the ingredients, in the large cup and pulse until smooth (bits of pine nuts are fine).
5. Return to the pan and reheat to serve.

NUTRITIONAL VALUES PER SERVING: 365 calories, 28.3g total fat, 6mg cholesterol, 592.5mg sodium, 753.8mg potassium, 20.7g carbohydrates, 4.8g fibre, 10.8g sugar, 9.6g protein.

Cherry Tomato and Basil Soup

Instead of using tinned tomatoes for this quick tomato soup we have used cherry tomatoes. Often with better flavour than larger tomatoes, especially out of season, these little tomatoes will become soft on the inside and charred on the outside when cooked in a frying pan. Paired with fresh basil, one of their natural partners, and olive oil to aid absorption of antioxidant nutrients, these little tomatoes make a quick, light and fresh tasting soup. For something a little creamier add a dollop of crème fraiche; it lends a pleasing acidity too.

SERVINGS: 1
PREPARATION TIME: 10 minutes
COOKING TIME: 10 minutes

INGREDIENTS

1 tbsp. olive oil
300 g cherry tomatoes
2 pinches sea salt
8 leaves fresh basil
Plenty freshly ground black
    pepper

1. Heat the oil in a frying pan and add the tomatoes.

2. Cook over a high heat, shaking the pan occasionally, for about 10 minutes or until the tomatoes have softened and charred slightly around the outside.

3. Add salt and pepper and set aside to cool; just for 5 or 10 minutes.

4. Place the tomatoes with a little more olive oil and the basil leaves into the large cup. Blend until smooth.

5. Return to the pan to heat and serve hot with a spoonful of crème fraiche if you want a creamy version.

NUTRITIONAL VALUES PER SERVING: 180 calories, 14.4g total fat, 0mg cholesterol, 589.2mg sodium, 629mg potassium, 13.2g carbohydrates, 3.2g fibre, <1g sugar, 2.5g protein.

Courgette, Mint, Dill, and Mange Tout

Peas, including the varieties eaten in the pod, are actually legumes rather than vegetables. As such, they provide protein and B vitamins as well as a range of essential minerals. Frozen peas, straight to the freezer from harvesting are more likely to be fresh than those sold as fresh. Fresh green peas are also a good source of vitamin C. This soup will benefit from the flavour of chicken stock as the ingredients are only briefly cooked so have not had time to develop depth of flavour. The mint and the dill suit the peas and courgettes particularly well.

SERVINGS: 1
PREPARATION TIME: 10 minutes
COOKING TIME: 10 minutes

INGREDIENTS

1 tbsp. olive oil
1 small courgette, diced
50 g mange tout
1 pinch salt
1 tbsp. mint, chopped
2 tbsp. dill, chopped
250 ml stock

1. Heat the oil in a frying pan and add the vegetables with a pinch of salt. Seasoning whilst cooking not only helps the food to break down, but achieves greater depth of flavour in the dish. The only time you should be salting at the end is when you check the seasoning and find it to be lacking.

2. Stir fry over a high heat for about 5 minutes and set aside the pan to cool slightly.

3. Place the vegetables in the large cup with the rest of the ingredients and pulse until smooth.

4. Reheat to serve.

NUTRITIONAL VALUES PER SERVING: 252 calories, 17g total fat, 7.5mg cholesterol, 662.3mg sodium, 694.5mg potassium, 16.5g carbohydrates, 2.6g fibre, 8.9g sugar, 9.3g protein.

Pea, Cucumber, and Dill

As well as ideal for chilled soups, cucumber is surprisingly good in hot soups too and can be interesting when cooked. Largely due to its water content, but also because its own skin is full of antioxidant nutrients, cucumber is great for skin health. A good source of vitamin C and folic acid, cucumber is also an important source of silica; essential for strong connective tissues.

SERVINGS: 1
PREPARATION TIME: 10 minutes
COOKING TIME: 10 minutes

INGREDIENTS

1 tbsp. olive oil
50 g frozen peas
½ cucumber, chopped
½ clove garlic
1 pinch salt
2 tbsp. fresh dill
Freshly ground black pepper
200 ml water or stock

1. Heat the oil in a frying pan and add the cucumber and peas with a pinch of salt and the garlic clove.

2. Stir fry for a few minutes before removing from the heat and fishing out the garlic.

3. Place the cooked vegetables in the large cup with the rest of the ingredients and pulse until smooth

4. Reheat to serve.

NUTRITIONAL VALUES PER SERVING: 181 calories, 14g total fat, 0mg cholesterol, 354.7mg sodium, 309.1mg potassium, 11.2g carbohydrates, 3.6g fibre, 4.7g sugar, 3.7g protein.

Watercress and Walnut Soup

Watercress is a great alternative to the ubiquitous rocket or other green leaves with its fresh peppery taste and crisp texture. Surprisingly, it is as nutritious as kale; full of fibre, vitamin C and vitamin E to name a few of its benefits. Here we keep it simple, and no-cook apart from heating, with a handful of walnuts and chicken stock; a spoonful of crème fraiche makes for creamy luxury that the peppery watercress, in this instance, needs. Think watercress sauce in soup form.

SERVINGS: 1
PREPARATION TIME: 15 minutes

INGREDIENTS

50 g watercress
2 tbsp. walnuts
1 pinch salt
200 ml chicken stock
2 tbsp. crème fraiche

1. Pulse all of the ingredients in the large cup with the extractor blade until smooth.

2. Slowly reheat to serve.

NUTRITIONAL VALUES PER SERVING: 222 calories, 17g total fat, 18.5mg cholesterol, 616.7mg sodium, 475mg potassium, 10.5g carbohydrates, 1.3g fibre, 4.3g sugar, 9g protein.

THICK AND CREAMY SOUPS

These soups have a more robust texture than their super smooth counterparts, and ingredients that lend themselves well to a creamier finish. Depending on your dietary outlook, potatoes may be frowned upon or embraced, but it cannot be denied that they bring a wonderful texture to soups; with the powerful blades of the NutriBullet you can leave the skins on and benefit from all the nutrients within.

Artichoke with Peas and Lemon

Artichokes are enormously nutritious but often overlooked unless part of an antipasti type platter. Raw artichokes are difficult to find and fiddly to prepare so this easy soup uses the tinned version. You can use frozen peas as well which means this really is a blitz and go. A touch of lemon brightens the palate whilst parsley introduces a fresh element; oil is added, even though no cooking is involved, to add body and nutrient value to the dish. Getting enough fat is an important part of any healthy diet and will help you absorb nutrients and stay full for longer.

SERVINGS: 1
PREPARATION TIME: 10 minutes
TOTAL TIME: 10 minutes

INGREDIENTS

200 g tinned artichokes
50 g frozen peas, defrosted
1 pinch salt
1 tbsp. olive oil
1 squeeze lemon juice
2 tbsp. parsley
Freshly ground black pepper

1. Pulse all of the ingredients in the large cup with the extractor blade until smooth.

2. Slowly reheat to serve.

NUTRITIONAL VALUES PER SERVING: 264 calories, 14.1g total fat, 0mg cholesterol, 530.8mg sodium, 843.5mg potassium, 30.6g carbohydrates, 13.5g fibre, 2.7g sugar, 9.9g protein.

Asian Broccoli Soup

A simple pureed soup of broccoli is enhanced, both nutritionally and flavour wise, with the addition of ginger, chilli and a splash of coconut milk. Broccoli is one of the most nutritious vegetables out there with its high vitamin C content and quota of minerals. Most important however are the phytochemical compounds that deliver anti-cancer benefits and activate detoxification enzymes as well as helping macular degeneration. Eating broccoli several times a week is one of the best things you can do for your health.

SERVINGS: 1
PREPARATION TIME: 10 minutes
COOKING TIME: 10 minutes

INGREDIENTS

1 tbsp. olive oil
25 mm ginger, sliced
1 clove garlic, sliced
1 red chilli, chopped
1 head broccoli, in florets
1 tbsp. coconut oil
1 tbsp. soy sauce
100 ml coconut milk
100 ml stock or water

1. Heat the oil in a sauce pan and add the chilli, ginger and garlic. Turn the heat down, cover and cook for 5 minutes, stirring occasionally.

2. Remove from the heat and lift the lid.

3. Add the broccoli with the rest of the ingredients to the large cup and pulse until smooth, yet still textured.

4. Reheat to serve.

NUTRITIONAL VALUES PER SERVING: 717 calories, 51.9g total fat, 3mg cholesterol, 894.2mg sodium, 2455.8mg potassium, 56.2g carbohydrates, 16.7g fibre, 14.6g sugar, 23.2g protein.

Broccoli, Leek, and Tarragon

Broccoli is more nutritious when eaten raw but the texture when made into soup is not particularly palatable and the flavour is quite bitter. Here, as a compromise, we cook it briefly to release the flavours and break down the fibres a little; it also deepens the vibrant green colour. With the added softness of leeks and the unmistakable anise tones of tarragon this is an interesting as well as nutritious soup.

SERVINGS: 1
PREPARATION TIME: 10 minutes
COOKING TIME: 10 minutes

INGREDIENTS

½ head broccoli, finely sliced stalks and small florets
½ leek, green and white, chopped
1 tbsp. tarragon
1 pinch sea salt
1 tbsp. olive oil
200 ml stock or water
1 crème fraiche
Freshly ground black pepper

1. Heat the oil in a saucepan and add the leek and broccoli, stems included. Add salt and cook over a gentle heat for 5 minutes until the broccoli is deep green and slightly tender, and the leeks soft.

2. Put the contents of the pan in the large cup with the stock or water and pulse until thick and blended but not smoothly pureed.

3. Return to the pan with the crème fraiche, a good twist of black pepper, and heat to serve.

NUTRITIONAL VALUES PER SERVING: 241 calories, 17.2g total fat, 8.5mg cholesterol, 591mg sodium, 435.7mg potassium, 16g carbohydrates, 1g fibre, 5g sugar, 7g protein.

Courgette and Sweetcorn Chowder

Courgette and sweetcorn are an excellent combination as they each offset the qualities of the other; sweet corn softens the bitter edge of the courgette whilst in turn the courgette stops the corn on the right side of sweet. Parsley adds it fresh herbal edge, whilst tarragon brings a slight hint of anise that pairs particularly well with courgette.

SERVINGS: 1
PREPARATION TIME: 10 minutes
COOKING TIME: 10 minutes

INGREDIENTS

1 courgette, diced
1 tbsp. olive oil
1 pinch salt
½ small tin sweetcorn
2 tbsp. parsley
1 tbsp. tarragon
200 ml stock
Freshly ground black pepper

1. Heat the oil in a saucepan and add the courgette with a pinch of salt.

2. Fry gently for 5 minutes until the courgette begins to soften.

3. Remove from the heat and add to the large cup with the rest of the ingredients. Pulse until it half blended and the ingredients are still separately visible.

4. Reheat to serve.

NUTRITIONAL VALUES PER SERVING: 272 calories, 17g total fat, 6mg cholesterol, 720.6mg sodium, 930.6mg potassium, 24g carbohydrates, 3.7g fibre, 9.9g sugar, 9.2g protein.

Mushroom, Thyme, and Walnut Soup

This soup is perfect for the unique properties of the NutriBullet and gives a quick, deeply savoury soup in just twenty minutes. Mushrooms are bursting with minerals; selenium, copper, potassium and zinc. They also have unique anti-cancer properties too. Walnuts provide essential omega-3 fatty acids as well as vitamin E and magnesium whilst a shot of fresh parsley offers minerals, vitamin C and carotenes.

SERVINGS: 1
PREPARATION TIME: 10 minutes
COOKING TIME: 10 minutes

INGREDIENTS

6 white mushrooms, cleaned and quartered (see note)
1/4 white onion, roughly chopped
1 clove garlic, crushed
1 sprig fresh thyme
1 tbsp. walnut oil
1 pinch flaked sea salt
200 ml water
2 tbsp. fresh parsley
2 tbsp. walnuts
1 tbsp. crème fraiche (optional)
Freshly ground black pepper

1. Clean the mushrooms; without water. Chop the unpeeled mushrooms into rough quarters, chop the onion into chunks and crush the garlic.

2. Put the mushrooms, garlic and onion into the large NutriBullet cup. Add the thyme and oil. Blitz the contents of the large cup, using the extractor blade.

4. Heat a pan over a medium heat and scrape in the mushroom mixture. Add salt and pepper then cook, stirring, for about five minutes.

5. Meanwhile, with the small cup and the milling blade, blitz the walnuts and parsley together to form a coarse crumb. Set aside

6. Add the water to the pan and let it heat to almost boiling point. Stir in the walnut and parsley mixture, along with the crème fraiche if using. Check your seasoning and serve hot.

NUTRITIONAL VALUES PER SERVING: 288 calories, 26.3g total fat, 6.2mg cholesterol, 318.4mg sodium, 552.4mg potassium, 11.1g carbohydrates, 3.3g fibre, 4.3g sugar, 6.8g protein.

Potato and Watercress Soup

Creamy cooked potato is blended in the NutriBullet with peppery raw watercress to create a classic blend of flavours with all the nutritional power of this vibrant green water plant. Often overlooked in favour of rocket or other bitter green leaves, watercress is a wonderful addition to your nutritional arsenal.

SERVINGS: 1
PREPARATION TIME: 10 minutes
COOKING TIME: 15 minutes

INGREDIENTS

1 potato, unpeeled and diced
1 pinch sea salt
1 tbsp. olive oil
200 ml stock or water
50 g watercress

1. Heat the oil in a saucepan and add the potatoes and salt. Cook over a gentle heat for a few minutes and then add a third of the stock or water. Cover the pan and simmer gently for 10 minutes until the potato is cooked.

2. Put all of the ingredients into the large cup (the cold liquid and the watercress will offset any heat from the potatoes) and pulse until smooth.

3. Return to the pan and reheat to serve.

NUTRITIONAL VALUES PER SERVING: 339 calories, 16.1g total fat, 6mg cholesterol, 599.8mg sodium, 1149.8mg potassium, 39.9g carbohydrates, 4.3g fibre, 4.7g sugar, 9.9g protein.

Potato, Parsley, and Parmesan Soup

Herbs such as parsley, with their high chlorophyll content, have such great nutritional value but are often used in such small amounts. Here, the parsley is the star, softened by creamy potato and given a savoury edge with freshly grated Parmesan.

SERVINGS: 1
PREPARATION TIME: 10 minutes
COOKING TIME: 15 minutes

INGREDIENTS

1 potato, unpeeled and diced
1 pinch sea salt
1 tbsp. olive oil
200 ml stock or water
50 g parsley; leaves
    and stalks
15 g Parmesan, freshly
    grated
Freshly ground black pepper

1. Heat the oil in a saucepan and add the potatoes and salt. Cook over a gentle heat for a few minutes and then add a third of the stock or water. Cover the pan and simmer gently for 10 minutes until the potato is cooked.

2. Put all of the ingredients into the large cup and pulse until smooth.

3. Return to the pan, add the Parmesan and plenty of black pepper, then reheat to serve.

NUTRITIONAL VALUES PER SERVING: 339 calories, 16.1g total fat, 6mg cholesterol, 599.8mg sodium, 1149.8mg potassium, 39.9g carbohydrates, 4.3g fibre, 4.7g sugar, 9.9g protein.

Roasted Cauliflower, Mint, and Hazelnut

A subtle soup of roasted cauliflower is garnished with a crumb of raw cauliflower, mint, and hazelnuts; both elements of which can made with ease in your NutriBullet.

SERVINGS: 1
PREPARATION TIME: 10 minutes
COOKING TIME: 20 minutes

INGREDIENTS

1 small cauliflower,
   in florets with stalk
   reserved.
1 tbsp. olive oil
1 pinch sea salt
2 tbsp. raw hazelnuts
2 tbsp. fresh mint
200 ml chicken stock
   or water

1. Preheat the oven to 200°C.

2. Place the cauliflower florets on a roasting tray with the oil and salt. Roast for 20 minutes until brown and slightly tender.

3. Meanwhile, add the nuts, mint and cauliflower stalks to the small cup and pulse with the milling blade to form a coarse crumb.

4. Add the stock or water to the large cup with the roasted cauliflower and stock or water. Pulse until smooth.

5. Place in a saucepan and heat to serve.

6. Garnish with the mint crumb.

NUTRITIONAL VALUES PER SERVING: 616 calories, 51.1g total fat, 6mg cholesterol, 648.8mg sodium, 1406.3mg potassium, 30.2g carbohydrates, 11.1g fibre, 10.7g sugar, 18.7g protein.

SUPER SMOOTH SOUPS

This section includes the soups that are light, yet comforting. Blended right down to a puree, many feature just one or two key flavours. There is no quicker way to a muddy soup than throwing too many ingredients at it and then pureeing it down. Where possible the ingredients have been included raw, or a mixture of raw and cooked. Cooked vegetables have been prepared in such a way as to maximise flavour and nutrient value.

Beetroot, Apple, and Hazelnut

Beetroots are more nutritious when eaten raw, yet raw soups have a texture more like a smoothie that does not always translate well into our idea of soup. Here we use a blend of cooked and raw beetroot to give the best of both worlds; a trick that actually results in more layers of flavour too. The cooked beetroot is deep, sweet and earthy, whilst the raw beet is more vibrant and alive. Raw apple complements the beetroot well, whilst toasted hazelnuts lend a bitter caramel and a sophisticated air.

SERVINGS: 1
PREPARATION TIME: 15 minutes
COOKING TIME: 50 minutes

INGREDIENTS

2 small beetroots; organic are best
1 pinch salt
1 tbsp. olive oil
1 eating apple, roughly chopped
3 tbsp. raw hazelnuts
200 ml water

1. Preheat the oven to 200°C.

2. Cut the beets into quarters and put half on a roasting tray; it really is worth roasting extra to justify turning the oven on. Or roast a chicken at the same time.

3. Drizzle with oil, sprinkle with salt and roast for about 40 minutes. Beets can be a bit odd as they don't feel done but actually are. Insert a sharp knife to make sure; it will be firmer than you imagine.

4. For the last 5 minutes, put the hazelnuts on the tray to roast; keep an eye that they don't burn. Remove the tray from the oven and leave for 5 minutes to cool.

6. Add the raw beets and apple to the large cup with half of the water and pulse.

7. Now add the rest of the water with the cooked beets and apple. Blend until smooth and transfer to a pan. Check your seasoning and heat to serve.

NUTRITIONAL VALUES PER SERVING: 768 calories, 65.6g total fat, 0mg cholesterol, 376.4mg sodium, 1053.2mg potassium, 42.8g carbohydrates, 14.4g fibre, 24.8g sugar, 14.7g protein.

Butter Bean Puree with Emerald Mint Oil

A thick and satisfying soup with plenty of protein and fibre from the beans to really fill you up. Kept simple with some cooked onions and garlic for depth, the soup is garnished simply with a deep emerald mint oil for a real flavour twist. Super easy, all you need to do is fry a few onions and blitz the rest. Fresh mint contains anti-cancer compounds and is said to prevent against allergies. It also delivers a fresh blast from the volatile essential oil menthol.

SERVINGS: 1
PREPARATION TIME: 10 minutes
COOKING TIME: 5 minutes

INGREDIENTS

1 tsp olive oil
½ onion, chopped
1 clove garlic, chopped
1 pinch sea salt
½ tin butter beans
200 ml stock

FOR THE MINT OIL

1 small bunch mint
50 ml olive oil

1. Fry the onions and garlic in the oil with a pinch of salt, until sweated down and beginning to brown.

2. Place all of the soup ingredients in the large cup and pulse with the extractor blade until smooth.

3. In the small cup, pulse the mint with the oil until smooth.

4. Reheat the soup to serve and garnish with a generous drizzle of mint oil; the rest can be kept in the fridge for a few days.

NUTRITIONAL VALUES PER SERVING: 723 calories, 53.4g total fat, 6mg cholesterol, 1131mg sodium, 896.8mg potassium, 46.6g carbohydrates, 12.9g fibre, 9.8g sugar, 17.4g protein.

Butternut Squash, Bacon, and Pecan

Full of carotenes, butternut squash is an essential part of any cancer prevention programme. Here it is made into a smooth soup, intensified by the savoury edge of bacon and garnished with a sage and pecan crumb. A drizzle of maple syrup really rounds the flavours out. Enjoy!

SERVINGS: 1
PREPARATION TIME: 10 minutes
COOKING TIME: 20 minutes

INGREDIENTS

1 tbsp. rapeseed oil
2 rashers back bacon,
    chopped
½ onion, chopped
¼ butternut squash peeled
    and cut into 25 mm cubes
4 leaves fresh sage
1 tbsp. pecans
200 ml water
1 pinch sea salt
Freshly ground black pepper
1 drizzle maple syrup

1. Heat the oil in a saucepan and add the bacon with the onion. Fry for 1 or 2 minutes until the bacon is beginning to brown and the onion softening.

2. Add the squash and 2 sage leaves, turn the heat down, cover, and cook for 10 minutes, checking and stirring regularly; if it shows signs of catching add a few tbsp. of water now and again to create steam.

3. Once the squash is just tender, remove the pan from the heat and fish out the sage.

4. Whilst it cools enough to go in the NutriBullet, put the pecan nuts, 2 sage leaves and a good pinch of salt in the small cup. Pulse with the milling blade to a coarse crumb.

5. Add the contents of the pan to the large cup and add the rest of the water. Pulse until the squash is smooth, but leaving bits of bacon in the mix.

6. Return the soup to the pan, season generously with black pepper, and heat to serve. Garnish with the pecan crumb and a scant drizzle of maple syrup.

NUTRITIONAL VALUES PER SERVING: 468 calories, 41.5g total fat, 37mg cholesterol, 657.9mg sodium, 440.7mg potassium, 16.7g carbohydrates, 3g fibre, 6.3g sugar, 9.2g protein.

Carrot, Almond and Cumin

The beneficial compounds in carrots, carotenes, are made more accessible through cooking. Nutrient dense almonds add not only minerals and vitamin E but nutty depth to the flavour of the soup whilst cumin lends an exotic air as well as assisting digestion.

SERVINGS: 1
PREPARATION TIME: 10 minutes
COOKING TIME: 20 minutes

INGREDIENTS

2 carrots
1 tbsp. olive oil
1 pinch sea salt
2 tbsp. whole almonds
1 tsp cumin seeds
200 ml water

1. Preheat the oven to 180°C.

2. Leave the carrots unpeeled and chop into coarse wedges. Reserve a chunk for garnish if desired.

3. Roast the carrots with a little oil and salt for about 20 minutes until they soften and brown.

4. In a dry saucepan, toast the almonds with the cumin seeds until the smell rises up.

5. Add the carrots, cumin and almonds to the large cup, add 200 ml of water, and pulse to smooth with the extractor blade.

6. Return to the pan to heat, check your seasoning, and serve with a garnish of grated carrot, chopped almond and fresh coriander if desired.

NUTRITIONAL VALUES PER SERVING: 262 calories, 20.2g total fat, 0mg cholesterol, 403.5mg sodium, 641mg potassium, 19g carbohydrates, 6.2 g fibre, 8.2g sugar, 4.4g protein.

Celeriac, Orange, and Thyme

Celeriac is often overlooked, perhaps due to its somewhat unappetising appearance or due to lack of knowledge about how to deal with it. Celeriac, like its shoots (celery), is also underestimated in the nutrition department; an excellent source of coumarins. These powerful plants are helpful in cancer prevention and also in vascular health. Celeriac is not as intensely flavoured as celery and sweetens with cooking; here we lift the flavours with freshly squeezed orange juice and the herbal scent of thyme.

SERVINGS: 1
PREPARATION TIME: 10 minutes
COOKING TIME: 30 minutes

INGREDIENTS

1 tbsp. rapeseed oil
¼ medium celeriac, peeled and chopped into cubes.
1 small potato, chopped into chunks
½ onion, chopped
1 clove garlic, peeled but whole
1 sprig thyme
1 pinch sea salt
½ orange, juice only
Freshly ground black pepper
250 ml water or stock
1 tsp crème fraiche

1. Heat the oil in a saucepan and add the celeriac, potato, onion, garlic, thyme and salt.

2. Cook gently over a low heat for 10 minutes, stirring often, and watching that it doesn't cook too quickly or burn.

3. After 10 minutes, add half of the water, cover the pan, and cook for another 10 minutes or until the veg are soft. Remove from the heat and leave aside to cool.

5. When the contents of the pan are cool enough to stick your finger in comfortably add them to the large cup with the orange juice and the rest of the water. Pulse with the extractor blade until smooth.

6. Return to the pan and heat. Check seasoning, stir the crème fraiche and serve hot.

NUTRITIONAL VALUES PER SERVING: 331 calories, 15.1g total fat, 2.5mg cholesterol, 346.9mg sodium, 1051.3mg potassium, 46g carbohydrates, 6.4g fibre, 8.4g sugar, 5.5g protein.

Curried Cauliflower Soup

Cauliflower may not be quite as nutritious as its other relatives on the cruciferous family as it lacks chlorophyll. It still delivers a substantial range of nutrients however and is one of the only vegetable sources of the mineral boron. Other vital nutrients include vitamin K, vitamin C and potassium. Cauliflower has a wonderful nutty depth when cooked as well as a creamy flavour; it can also take on other robust flavours yet retain its unique character. Here it forms the base of a creamy comforting soup with an added kiss of mild curry spices.

SERVINGS: 1
PREPARATION TIME: 10 minutes
COOKING TIME: 20 minutes

INGREDIENTS

1 small cauliflower, broken
   into florets
1 tbsp. olive oil
1 pinch sea salt
2 tsp curry powder
250 ml stock or water

1. Preheat the oven to 200°C.

2. Toss the cauliflower in the salt, spices and oil then place on a baking tray.

3. Roast for about 20 minutes until browned and cooked through, but still with a little bite.

4. Put the cauliflower and the stock into the large cup and pulse to smooth.

5. Return to the pan and heat to serve.

NUTRITIONAL VALUES PER SERVING: 290 calories, 17.8g total fat, 7.6mg cholesterol, 726.5mg sodium, 1120.5mg potassium, 24.5g carbohydrates, 6.6g fibre, 9.2g sugar, 12g protein.

Double Carrot Coriander

A souped up version of the classic carrot and coriander we use raw and cooked carrot in this soup as well as coriander leaf and seeds. Carrots are the best source of provitamin A carotenes (the nutrients that the body converts to vitamin A) and are excellent in the fight against macular degeneration as well as preventing against heart disease and cancer.

SERVINGS: 1
PREPARATION TIME: 10 minutes
COOKING TIME: 30 minutes

INGREDIENTS

3 carrots, unpeeled and chopped. Leave a little grated for garnish.
1 tbsp. coconut oil
1 pinch sea salt
1 tbsp. coriander seed
2 tbsp. coriander leaf, with a little extra for garnish
200 ml stock or water

1. Preheat the oven to 200°C.

2. Roast the carrots in the coconut oil for roughly 20 minutes.

3. Place all of the ingredients in the large cup and pulse until smooth.

4. Reheat to serve and garnish with grated carrot and coriander leaf.

NUTRITIONAL VALUES PER SERVING: 306 calories, 17.5g total fat, 6mg cholesterol, 742.4mg sodium, 1098.7mg potassium, 33.5g carbohydrates, 9.2g fibre, 14.7g sugar, 8.1g protein.

Fennel and Leek

Roasted fennel and leeks make the perfect partners, with the addition of fennel seeds for an extra flavour boost. Fennel is a good source of fibre and essential minerals as well as vitamin C. Leeks deliver the same nutrient benefits as garlic and onion; as such they are anti-bacterial, fighting against infection, and full of anti-cancer compounds.

SERVINGS: 1
PREPARATION TIME: 10 minutes
COOKING TIME: 30 minutes

INGREDIENTS

2 small fennel bulbs,
   cut into wedges
1 leek, cut into 50 mm
   sections
½ tsp fennel seed
1 pinch sea salt
1 tbsp. olive oil
250 ml stock or water

1. Preheat the oven to 200°C.

2. Lay the fennel with the leeks on a baking tray, drizzle with oil and sprinkle with sea salt.

3. Roast for about 20 minutes or until just soft. Set aside to cool slightly

4. Put the ingredients in the large cup, with the stock or water, and pulse until smooth.

5. Put the soup in a saucepan to heat and check the seasoning.

NUTRITIONAL VALUES PER SERVING: 321 calories, 18.5g total fat, 7.7mg cholesterol, 1415mg sodium, 1065.2mg potassium, 35.6g carbohydrates, 8.2g fibre, 3.5g sugar, 7g protein.

Fennel with Pomegranate

The fennel takes a little longer in the oven but takes on a beautifully sweet depth when cooked in this way. A very simple soup, with a few key ingredients, it does benefit from using chicken stock instead of water but don't worry if water is all you have. Try to get fennel bulbs that still have their lacy fronds atop; they make a pretty garnish and add an extra layer of fresh flavour. The subtle smoothness of the soup is brought into sharp contrast by a stunning garnish of pink pomegranate seeds and parsley oil.

SERVINGS: 1
PREPARATION TIME: 10 minutes
COOKING TIME: 30 minutes

INGREDIENTS

2 small fennel bulbs,
   cut into wedges
1 pinch sea salt
1 tbsp. olive oil
250 ml stock or water
1 tbsp. pomegranate seeds
For the parsley oil
2 tbsp. walnut oil
1 handful parsley leaves

1. Preheat the oven to 200°C.

2. Lay the fennel on a baking tray, drizzle with oil and sprinkle with sea salt.

3. Roast for about 20 minutes or until just soft. Set aside to cool slightly.

4. To make the parsley oil, put the parsley and walnut oil in the small cup and pulse with the milling blade until completely smooth.

5. Put the fennel in the large cup, with the stock or water, and pulse until smooth.

6. Put the soup in a saucepan to heat and check the seasoning.

7. Serve hot with a drizzle of the parsley oil and a spoonful of pomegranate seeds.

8. Keep the rest of the oil in the fridge and use within a few days to flavour soups, dressings, sandwiches; all manner of things really.

NUTRITIONAL VALUES PER SERVING: 305 calories, 22.6g total fat, 7.7mg cholesterol, 1398.5mg sodium, 909.1mg potassium, 22.8g carbohydrates, 6.3g fibre, <1g sugar, 5.6g protein.

Moroccan Carrot Soup

The beneficial compounds in carrots, carotenes, are made more accessible through cooking and the textures are perfect for all manner of soups. Here we roast the carrots for depth of flavour, with added spices for an exotic dish, and serve with a garnish of raw carrot, raisins, and yoghurt.

SERVINGS: 1
PREPARATION TIME: 10 minutes
COOKING TIME: 20 minutes

INGREDIENTS

2 carrots, unpeeled and chopped with some grated for garnish
1 tbsp. olive oil
1 pinch sea salt
1 tsp turmeric
1 tsp ground allspice
1 tsp cumin seeds
1 tsp raisins
1 tbsp. low fat natural yoghurt
200 ml water

1. Preheat the oven to 180°C.

2. Roast the carrots with the oil, spices and salt for about 20 minutes until they soften and brown.

3. Add the carrots to the large cup, add 200 ml of water, and pulse to smooth with the extractor blade.

4. Return to the pan to heat, check your seasoning, and serve with a garnish of grated carrot, raisins and a swirl of yoghurt.

NUTRITIONAL VALUES PER SERVING: 225 calories, 132 calories from fat, 15g total fat, <1mg cholesterol, 417mg sodium, 691.6mg potassium, 22.7g carbohydrates, 5.7g fibre, 9.6g sugar, 3.1g protein.

Potato, Leek, and Parmesan

This is a real comfort soup; smooth and soulful with delicate creamy flavours. Leeks have a real affinity with butter but you could use olive oil instead if you wish. You could also omit the parmesan, but again it adds real flavour to the soup. Use chicken stock, if you have it, for a rich rounded taste; water will happily suffice if not.

SERVINGS: 1
PREPARATION TIME: 10 minutes
COOKING TIME: 20 minutes

INGREDIENTS

1 leek, chopped
1 tsp olive oil
1 tsp butter
1 pinch salt
1 small potato, unpeeled and diced
250 ml stock or water
1 tbsp. parmesan, grated

1. Sauté the leek and potato in the oil and butter (the oil prevents the butter from burning) with a pinch of salt. Keep the heat low and stir often.

2. After about ten minutes, when the ingredients have softened and browned, add a few tbsp. of stock or water and let it boil.

3. Remove the pan from the heat, cover, and leave to stand until the potatoes are soft.

4. Remove the lid and leave to cool for 10 minutes.

5. Add the contents of the pan, with the cold stock or water, to the large cup and pulse until smooth.

6. Return to the pan and heat to serve.

7. Garnish with freshly grated parmesan.

NUTRITIONAL VALUES PER SERVING: 372 calories, 13.2g total fat, 22.2mg cholesterol, 758.4mg sodium, 1149.7mg potassium, 51.5g carbohydrates, 5.3g fibre, 8.9g sugar, 13.1g protein.

Roasted Parsnip
and Curried Apple Soup

Nutritionally speaking, the humble apple is one of the most overlooked fruits around; packed with soluble fibre, important phytochemicals, and potassium. Best eaten raw, with their skin, apples provide sweetness in place of refined sugar yet also a refreshing sharpness too. Paired here with roasted parsnip, the raw dessert apple prevents the sweet root form being overly cloying whilst a spoonful of curry powder keeps it simple but brings plenty of flavour. A garnish of crisp grated apple and a few raisins adds yet more interest to a lovely little soup.

SERVINGS: 1
PREPARATION TIME: 10 minutes
COOKING TIME: 30 minutes

INGREDIENTS

1 large parsnip
1 tbsp. olive oil
1 pinch sea salt
¼ onion, chopped
1 tsp curry powder
200 ml water
1 apple
1 tsp raisins

1. Preheat the oven to 180°C.

2. Leave the parsnip unpeeled and cut in half horizontally. Cut each piece into wedges.

3. Roast the parsnips, with a little oil and salt, for roughly 20 minutes until soft and golden.

4. Fry the onion in a little oil for a couple of minutes to soften and brown slightly. Stir in the curry powder and remove from the heat.

5. Put the roasted parsnips and the cooked onion into the large cup and add the water and half of the apple.

6. Pulse until smooth and return to the pan to heat. Check your seasoning and serve garnished with the other half of the apple (grated) and a few raisins.

NUTRITIONAL VALUES PER SERVING: 269 calories, 14.3g total fat, 0mg cholesterol, 298.9mg sodium, 497.3mg potassium, 37.4g carbohydrates, 7.9g fibre, 20.7g sugar, 1.8g protein.

Sea Spray Soup

An interesting soup using an increasingly popular ingredient; samphire. A saline seashore vegetable often served as a simple accompaniment to seafood, samphire is a rare source of iodine, otherwise only found in organ meats and table salt. Here, we cook it slightly to soften a little and blend with chicken stock to round out the flavours. Seasoned generously, it needs nothing more than a decadent garnish of pan fried scallops. Do use butter instead of oil as it really enhances the flavour.

SERVINGS: 1
PREPARATION TIME: 10 minutes
COOKING TIME: 10 minutes

INGREDIENTS

1 tbsp. butter
100 g samphire
200 g chicken stock
Freshly ground black pepper
1 squeeze lemon juice

FOR THE GARNISH

3 scallops
1 tbsp. butter
1 pinch sea salt

1. Melt the butter in a frying pan and add the samphire. Cover, place over a medium heat, and cook for about 8 minutes, shaking the pan occasionally.

2. Remove from the heat, take of the lid and allow to cool.

3. Add the samphire to the large cup with the stock, black pepper and squeeze of lemon. Pulse to smooth and transfer to a saucepan to reheat.

4. Heat the other tablespoon of butter in the same frying pan and cook the scallops for 2 minutes on each side. Slice each scallop and arrange over the hot soup to serve.

NUTRITIONAL VALUES PER SERVING: 345 calories, 26g total fat, 77.9mg cholesterol, 795.7mg sodium, 681.8mg potassium, 14.5g carbohydrates, <1g fibre, 3.8g sugar, 16.6g protein.

Simply Asparagus

Asparagus is more readily nutritious when cooked and this simple soup makes the best of its unique flavours. You really should be using stock to give it more body and a rounder taste. Other than that a drop of lemon juice and a good twist of black pepper is all you need to enjoy a nutritious and delicious soup. You could try it chilled too.

SERVINGS: 1
PREPARATION TIME: 10 minutes
COOKING TIME: 10 minutes

INGREDIENTS

½ bunch asparagus, chopped
1 tbsp. olive oil
1 pinch sea salt
1 squeeze lemon juice
200 ml chicken stock
Freshly ground black pepper

1. Heat the oil in a saucepan and add the asparagus with a pinch of salt.

2. Cook gently over a low heat for 5 minutes until the asparagus is browned and slightly soft. Remove from the heat, cover and stand for 5 minutes.

3. Put the asparagus in the large cup with the stock and pulse until smooth.

4. Return to the pan and reheat to serve, adding a drop of lemon and a good grind of pepper to lift the flavours.

NUTRITIONAL VALUES PER SERVING: 209 calories, 16g total fat, 6mg cholesterol, 569.9mg sodium, 358.7mg potassium, 10.8g carbohydrates, 1.7g fibre, 4.5g sugar, 6.6g protein.

Squash, Coconut, and Chilli

A creamy blend of squash and coconut milk with the kick of chilli and a boost of lime. Although coconut contains saturated fats, their structure means that they are health promoting fats rather than something to be avoided. Coconuts are also rich in essential minerals.

SERVINGS: 1
PREPARATION TIME: 10 minutes
COOKING TIME: 30 minutes

INGREDIENTS

½ butternut squash, peeled and cut into 25 mm cubes
1 tbsp. coconut oil
1 pinch salt
200 g coconut milk
1 red chilli
1 lime, juice only
2 tbsp. coriander leaf

1. Preheat the oven to 200°C.

2. Place the squash on a roasting tray with the oil and the salt. Roast for 20 minutes or until tender.

3. Place the coconut milk, squash, lime and chilli into the large cup and pulse until smooth. Add the coriander and pulse once to chop.

4. Return to the pan and heat to serve.

NUTRITIONAL VALUES PER SERVING: 599 calories, 56.7g total fat, 0mg cholesterol, 331.5mg sodium, 1071.9mg potassium, 29.3g carbohydrates, 4.9g fibre, 5.8g sugar, 6.6g protein.

WARMING BROTHS

Broth is all about the stock and the more richly flavoured stock, the better the soup. Like the classic chicken soup, these soups are reviving and restorative with as much vital goodness from the stock itself as the vegetables. Use meat or chicken broth, with as much flavour and nutrients from the bones as possible.

Caldo Verde

A traditional Portuguese broth, of stock, potatoes, garlic and kale, this is the kind of nourishment you want on a cold winter's day with the sniffles coming on. You need stock, although the original would have been made without it. Kale is full of nourishing goodies; vitamin E, vitamin C for those sniffles, and plenty of fibre. It also has lots of wonderful bitter green flavour that just feels good for you whilst remaining delicious.

SERVINGS: 1
PREPARATION TIME: 10 minutes
COOKING TIME: 20 minutes

INGREDIENTS

50 g shredded kale
2 cloves garlic, crushed
1 potato, skin on, diced
300 ml chicken stock
1 pinch salt
Freshly ground black pepper

1. Unfortunately, the NutriBullet sits this one out, but no selection of soup recipes would be complete without this wonderful soup.

2. Put all of the ingredients in a saucepan and bring to a simmer.

3. Cook for 20 minutes, until the kale is cooked and the potatoes are soft.

4. Serve hot.

NUTRITIONAL VALUES PER SERVING: 277 calories, 4.1g total fat, 9mg cholesterol, 861.6mg sodium, 1249mg potassium, 48.6g carbohydrates, 5.6g fibre, 6.9g sugar, 12.8g protein.

Fragrant Asian Broth

You will need meat or chicken stock for this dish as it forms the base of the flavours. The raw ingredients are placed at the bottom of a bowl, and the hot stock is poured over the top for a vibrant yet restorative broth. We have used Asian greens but you can use any type of deep green cabbage that you can get your hands on.

SERVINGS: 1
PREPARATION TIME: 10 minutes
TOTAL TIME: 10 minutes

INGREDIENTS

½ carrot, grated
2 tbsp. mixed beansprouts
1 Bok choi, finely shredded
50 g shredded cooked chicken
2 tbsp. basil leaf, chopped
2 tbsp. coriander leaf, chopped
1 star anise
25 mm ginger
1 clove garlic
1 tsp black peppercorns
250 ml well flavoured stock

1. Put the vegetables, herbs, chicken and star anise in the bottom of a large bowl.

2. In the small cup, with the milling blade, pulse the ginger, garlic and peppercorns; you may need a spoonful of cold stock to loosen it.

3. Stir the paste into the stock, heat and pour into the bowl.

4. Eat whilst steaming hot and fragrant.

NUTRITIONAL VALUES PER SERVING: 234 calories, 5.7g total fat, 50.1mg cholesterol, 457.3mg sodium, 850.9mg potassium, 21.9g carbohydrates, 4.4g fibre, 7g sugar, 24.7g protein.

Hot and Sour Coconut Soup

As the name suggests this coconut based soup is hot from chillies and sour from the addition of lime juice. Hugely restorative with all the health giving benefits of chillies, and ginger, this is another soup to have when you feel under the weather. Serve over rice or noodles for a more substantial dish.

SERVINGS: 1
PREPARATION TIME: 10 minutes
COOKING TIME: 10 minutes

INGREDIENTS

1 stalk lemongrass

25 mm ginger

2 red chillies

2 limes, juice only

2 Kaffir lime leaves

½ small bunch coriander

1 tbsp. Thai fish sauce

125 ml coconut milk

125 ml chicken stock

1. Add all of the ingredients to the large cup and pulse until completely blended.

2. Heat to serve.

NUTRITIONAL VALUES PER SERVING: 418 calories, 28.8g total fat, 3.8mg cholesterol, 219.4mg sodium, 1361.2mg potassium, 40.3g carbohydrates, 2.2g fibre, 7.3g sugar, 8.7g protein.

Kale, Ginger, and Sesame Soup

The very term broth indicates that you need a good stock as the basis of the soup; without broth in this soup, what you have is a bowl of ingredients in hot water. So the quality of your stock is vital in this recipe.

SERVINGS: 1
PREPARATION TIME: 10 minutes
COOKING TIME: 15 minutes

INGREDIENTS

1 clove garlic
4 spring onions
25 mm ginger
1 tbsp. sesame seeds
1 tbsp. soy sauce
1 tbsp. coconut oil
50 g kale, finely shredded
250 ml well flavoured stock

1. Put the garlic, onions, ginger, sesame seeds and soy into the small cup and pulse with the milling blade to a coarse paste.

2. Heat the oil in a saucepan and add the kale. Stir for a few minutes and then add the spice paste. Stir again for a few minutes more and then add the stock.

3. When the stock is almost at boiling point, serve the hot broth in a big bowl. Add more soy as desired.

NUTRITIONAL VALUES PER SERVING: 496 calories, 22.1g total fat, 7.5mg cholesterol, 931.1mg sodium, 1313.2mg potassium, 63.7g carbohydrates, 9.6g fibre, 25.1g sugar, 16.5g protein.

Leek, Onion, Garlic, and Parsley

The purpose of this soup is a triple whammy of the protective effects of the members of the allium family; leeks, onions and garlic. Rich with deep flavour, the ingredients are cooked down until soft and unguent; with added chicken broth and lots of fresh green parsley, this takes chicken soup for the soul to a whole new level. Eat a bowl of this several times a week to keep those winter colds at bay.

SERVINGS: 1
PREPARATION TIME: 15 minutes
COOKING TIME: 20 minutes

INGREDIENTS

1 tbsp. butter
1 onion, sliced
3 cloves garlic, whole
½ leek, chopped
1 pinch salt
Freshly ground black pepper
1 bay leaf
250 ml chicken stock

1. Melt the butter in a saucepan and add the onion, garlic, and leek with a pinch of salt. Turn the heat down and cook slowly for about 20 minutes until the ingredients are soft and glossy.

2. Put all of the ingredients in the large cup and pulse just until the onions and leeks are incorporated through the broth and the green flecks of parsley are clearly visible.

3. Reheat to serve.

NUTRITIONAL VALUES PER SERVING: 282 calories, 14.8g total fat, 38mg cholesterol, 665.1mg sodium, 561.3mg potassium, 29.6g carbohydrates, 3.1g fibre, 11g sugar, 9g protein.

Roasted Garlic and Green Herb Broth

Beef bone broth is the best base for this wonderful meal; another winter warmer and infection fighter to keep all of those colds at bay. The nutrient content of bone broth is essential for building energy and strength, whilst the garlic does its usual job of fighting infection. Added parsley brings some green nutrients into the mix. Plenty of black pepper really finishes it off perfectly.

SERVINGS: 1
PREPARATION TIME: 10 minutes
COOKING TIME: 1 hour

INGREDIENTS

2 heads garlic, whole
1 pinch salt
1 tbsp. olive oil
250 ml bone broth
½ bunch parsley
Plenty of black pepper

1. Preheat the oven to 180°C.
2. Drizzle the garlic cloves with oil and sprinkle with salt. Roast for an hour until really soft.
3. Add all of the ingredients to the large cup and pulse until smooth.
4. Serve piping hot with loads of black pepper.

NUTRITIONAL VALUES PER SERVING: 260 calories, 15.5g total fat, 0mg cholesterol, 1094mg sodium, 625.1mg potassium, 22.7g carbohydrates, 2.3g fibre, 1.6g sugar, 9.8g protein.

Savoy Cabbage, Sausage, and Caraway

You can use chicken or meat stock for this dish, which relies on the strength of the broth for its flavour. Although cabbage is full of vitamins and minerals it is the phytochemical content that cause it to really stand out nutritionally as one of the greatest foods for cancer prevention. We choose Savoy cabbage for its wonderful texture and flavour but you can use any cabbage you choose.

SERVINGS: 1
PREPARATION TIME: 10 minutes
COOKING TIME: 10 minutes

INGREDIENTS

50 mm raw chorizo
¼ head Savoy cabbage, shredded
250 ml stock

FOR THE PASTE

1 clove garlic, crushed
1/2 onion
1 tsp caraway seeds
1 tsp paprika
1 tbsp. olive oil
1 pinch salt
1/2 red pepper
1 tsp tomato puree

1. Put all of the ingredients for the paste into the small cup and pulse until smooth.

2. Heat a large saucepan over a medium heat, add the paste and stir for 1 minute.

3. Add the chorizo to the pan, stir for another minute, and then add the cabbage with the stock.

4. Simmer until the cabbage is soft, check your seasoning, and serve whilst piping hot.

NUTRITIONAL VALUES PER SERVING: 421 calories, 28.5g total fat, 52.7mg cholesterol, 1087.7mg sodium, 710.7mg potassium, 25.8g carbohydrates, 5.2g fibre, 11.1g sugar, 17.9g protein.

Thai Green Chicken Noodle

This hot and aromatic soup is wonderfully restorative and full of fabulous flavour. The NutriBullet is used to make a fragrant spice paste that is added to coconut milk, noodles and chicken to make a filling one bowl dish.

SERVINGS: 1
PREPARATION TIME: 10 minutes
COOKING TIME: 10 minutes

INGREDIENTS

200 ml coconut milk

2 lime leaves

1 sheet egg noodles

100 g cooked chicken, shredded

FOR THE SPICE PASTE

1 stalk lemongrass

25 mm ginger

1 clove garlic

2 red chillies

1 tsp cumin

½ lime, zest and juice

2 tbsp. coriander leaf

1 tbsp. fish sauce

1. Add all of the spice paste ingredients to the small cup and pulse to a coarse paste with the extractor blade.

2. Add the contents to a saucepan and bring to a boil.

3. Add the noodles and cook for 7 minutes until soft, but not soggy, add the chicken and serve immediately.

NUTRITIONAL VALUES PER SERVING: 866 calories, 50.1g total fat, 131.4mg cholesterol, 1537.9mg sodium, 1281.7mg potassium, 66.8g carbohydrates, 4.8g fibre, 6.7g sugar, 45.2g protein.

SAUCES

If you can make a soup in your NutriBullet, then you can make a sauce. Many of these sauces are based on classic dishes from around the world, whilst others are simply combinations of simple flavours and nutritious ingredients. A delicious and nutritious sauce can make all the difference to a simple piece of grilled meat, an interesting shape of pasta or filling grains such as quinoa, cous cous or rice, and you can alter the consistency or texture to suit your needs. Enjoy.

Anchovy and Herb Sauce

Anchovies are salty and deeply savoury as opposed to violently fishy so if you think that you don't like them then maybe give them one more try. Full of calcium and vital omega 3 fatty acids, anchovies are a good way of getting these vital nutrients without having to resort to blatant fish consumption. We up the green content with a good handful of parsley and use olive oil with lemon to bring it all together to form a vibrant sauce that sits perfectly against the background of carb laden pasta. Spaghetti is an excellent vehicle for this sauce.

SERVINGS: 2
PREPARATION TIME: 10 minutes
COOKING TIME: 10 minutes

INGREDIENTS

80 g anchovy fillets
1 small onion, chopped
1 clove garlic
4 tbsp. olive oil
1 lemon, juice only
½ bunch parsley

1. Heat 1 tbsp. of the oil in a saucepan and add the onions. Cook gently until they begin to soften, add the garlic and cook for a further minute.

2. Add the anchovies and stir for several minutes; the anchovies will start to break down, seemingly melting into the onions.

3. Put the anchovies into the small cup, with the rest of the ingredients and pulse with the extractor blade until amalgamated yet still discernibly chunky.

4. There is no need to reheat, simply toss through steaming hot pasta.

NUTRITIONAL VALUES PER SERVING: 357 calories, 31.2g total fat, 34mg cholesterol, 1478.4mg sodium, 419mg potassium, 8.8g carbohydrates, 1.3g fibre, 3.1g sugar, 12.7g protein.

Asparagus Sauce

This dish is at its best when made with cream, or at least butter. You can however use olive oil if you must. Asparagus are such a good source of nutrients though, with unique properties that given the choice between zero fat or some fat, then you should be choosing the latter every time. Rich in protein with anti-inflammatory properties, asparagus is also diuretic; a fact that makes them an excellent detox aid. They really require little else other than salt, pepper and a touch of lemon. A grating of parmesan over the top wouldn't go amiss either.

SERVINGS: 2
PREPARATION TIME: 10 minutes
COOKING TIME: 10 minutes

INGREDIENTS

1 bunch asparagus
1 pinch salt
1 squeeze lemon juice
Black pepper
100 ml water
50 ml double cream

1. Bend each spear of asparagus until it breaks and separate the tips from the woody ends. The tips can go into the boiling pasta water about 4 minutes before the end of cooking time and be drained along with the pasta.

2. The woody stalks need to be cooked before you can make a sauce with them. Using the water for the sauce, simmer the asparagus with the salt for about 6 minutes until tender. Set aside to cool slightly.

3. When cool enough to go in the NutriBullet, add them to the large cup with the rest of the ingredients (not the asparagus spears) and pulse until you have a creamy sauce.

4. Toss through the hot pasta and asparagus spears, reheating if necessary.

NUTRITIONAL VALUES PER SERVING: 58 calories, 4.8g total fat, 17.3mg cholesterol, 148.7mg sodium, 144.8mg potassium, 3.4g carbohydrates, 1.5g fibre, 1.2g sugar, 1.7g protein.

Caponata Style Sauce

To get the most nutritional value from aubergines, you need to eat the beautiful purple skin as it contains powerful antioxidant compounds that lower cholesterol. Many people are a little dubious about aubergine, probably due to bad experiences with it in the past. It is very easy to cook aubergine well but it is also very easy to get it wrong; the difference lying usually between oil or water. Water has no business around aubergines, but oil turns it into a gloriously soft melting ingredient that has no competition in the vegetable world. Get aubergine right and you will be converted for life. This sauce is based on a Sicilian stew known as Caponata; here we pulse it down a little to make a flavourful sauce for pasta.

SERVINGS: 2
PREPARATION TIME: 10 minutes
COOKING TIME: 20 minutes

INGREDIENTS

½ aubergine, diced
½ red onion, diced
1 stick celery, diced
3 tbsp. olive oil
1 tbsp. capers
10 green olives, pitted
½ tsp sugar
1 tsp white wine vinegar
200 ml light tomato sauce

1. Preheat the oven to 200°C.

2. Toss the vegetables in 1 tbsp. of olive oil and roast in the oven for 15 minutes, until soft and slightly brown.

3. Add the roasted vegetables to the large cup with the rest of the ingredients and pulse with the extractor blade to form a chunky sauce.

4. Reheat the sauce and toss through a chunky pasta such as penne.

NUTRITIONAL VALUES PER SERVING: 253 calories, 22.9g total fat, 0mg cholesterol, 332.5mg sodium, 331.9mg potassium, 12.8g carbohydrates, 5.1g fibre, 5.5g sugar, 1.8g protein.

Chilli and Garlic Sauce

This sauce is a version of Mexican salsa rojo, a red chilli sauce using the Mexican holy trinity of chillies; ancho, pasilla, guajillo. Dried chillies, of all sizes, are readily available online and can really make a difference to your spicy cooking with their different heat levels and nuances of flavour. Dried chillies need pre-soaking first and once reconstituted are used as fresh. Dried chillies give great depth of flavour whereas their fresh counterparts are all about fresh herbal tones. The nutritional benefits of chillies, dried or fresh, are endless. They are anti-inflammatory and analgesic, aid cardiovascular health and boost immunity, and get the metabolism going for improved digestion. Garlic brings many benefits to the party too with its infection fighting compounds.

SERVINGS: 4
PREPARATION TIME: 10 minutes
COOKING TIME: 10 minutes

INGREDIENTS

40 g ancho chilli, soaked
30 g pasilla chilli, soaked
30 g guajillo chilli, soaked
1 pinch sea salt
2 cloves garlic
1 pinch oregano
1 tsp ground cumin
2 tbsp. olive oil
100 g light tomato sauce

1. Put all of the ingredients into the large cup and pulse until you have a smooth sauce.

2. Place the sauce in a pan and simmer for 10 minutes.

3. You can use this sauce as it is (it will be hot) or as a base for other ideas. It can also be used cold as a condiment or dip. It will keep in the fridge for a week.

NUTRITIONAL VALUES PER SERVING: 74 calories, 7g total fat, 0mg cholesterol, 74mg sodium, 96.6mg potassium, 3g carbohydrates, <1g fibre, 1.4g sugar, <1g protein.

Classic Pesto

There are so many variations of pesto around now, often created by overzealous chefs who feel the need to be different rather than making classics really well, that it can be easy to forget that wonderful blend of basil, Parmesan and pine nuts. Pesto, classic or otherwise, can be tossed through pasta for an instant dinner, spread in a sandwich for a hit o flavour or used as a dressing. The fresh homemade version carries far more vibrant flavours than its bottled counterparts and is far more nutritious too.

SERVINGS: 4
PREPARATION TIME: 15 minutes
COOKING TIME: 1 minute

INGREDIENTS

30 g pine nuts
50 g basil
30 g Parmesan, grated
75 g olive oil
1 clove garlic

1. First, toast the pine nuts for a minute in a dry frying pan.

2. Add them, with the rest of the ingredients, to the large cup and pulse with the extractor blade until you have a coarse paste.

3. Keep in a screw top jar in the fridge for up to a week. As well as the myriad of ways described in the introduction, you could use it to pep up lightly steamed vegetables. Good nutrition is not about forcing down unpalatable food, rather finding ways to increase your intake of nutrient dense ingredients in ways that you enjoy.

NUTRITIONAL VALUES PER SERVING: 253 calories, 26.1g total fat, 6.6mg cholesterol, 115.8mg sodium, 94.2mg potassium, 1.9g carbohydrates, <1g fibre, <1g sugar, 4.4g protein.

Courgette and Mint Sauce

Here courgettes are pulsed down to a coarse paste and fried before serving; a little mint makes a fine companion. The texture makes the nutrients in the squash easy to metabolise and forms the base of the sauce. The deep green skin of courgette is full of anti-cancer compounds. A little crème fraiche is added for creamy texture, but without the finely chopped courgette much more would be required; a little compromise in the name of both nutrition and eating quality. Serve with a long pasta such as spaghetti, tagliatelle or even bucatini.

SERVINGS: 2
PREPARATION TIME: 15 minutes
COOKING TIME: 10 minutes

INGREDIENTS

2 small courgettes, roughly
    chopped
2 tbsp. olive oil
1 clove garlic, crushed
2 tbsp. fresh mint
50 ml stock or water
2 tbsp. crème fraiche

1. Put the courgettes in the large cup with a pinch of salt, the olive oil and the garlic. Add a little stock or water to loosen and pulse with the extractor blade until you have a coarse paste. Add the rest of the water, more or less, depending on how thick you want the final sauce. The water content of the courgettes will vary and as such alter the liquid requirements of the dish. You are looking for something the consistency of puréed onion.

2. Heat the contents in a hot frying pan, adding a tbsp. of olive oil if it doesn't sizzle; cook, stirring for around ten minutes then add the mint and the crème fraiche. Add plenty of freshly ground black pepper and check the salt.

3. Toss with hot pasta to serve.

NUTRITIONAL VALUES PER SERVING: 175 calories, 16.6g total fat, 7mg cholesterol, 55.8mg sodium, 366.4mg potassium, 5.6g carbohydrates, 1.3g fibre, 3.7g sugar, 2.5g protein.

Courgette, Lemon, and Pine Nut Sauce

This is a pesto like sauce that will sit well in the fridge for a week. We use raw courgettes, parsley and lots of lemon, alongside the classic pine nuts and Parmesan. Courgettes are often thought of as being nutritionally bare but eaten with the skin they are an excellent source of anti-cancer compounds. Parsley is one of the best sources of green chlorophyll, which is as healthy as it sounds. Herbs are notoriously under used; when adding herbs to a dish think in tablespoons (at least) rather than pinches.

SERVINGS: 4
PREPARATION TIME: 15 minutes
COOKING TIME: 1 minute

INGREDIENTS

1 courgette, chopped
2 lemons, zest only
30 g pine nuts
50 g parsley
30 g Parmesan, grated
75 g olive oil
1 clove garlic

1. First, toast the pine nuts for a minute in a dry frying pan.

2. Add them, with the rest of the ingredients, to the large cup and pulse with the extractor blade until you have a coarse paste.

3. Keep in a screw top jar in the fridge for up to a week. As well as the myriad of ways described in the introduction, you could use it to pep up lightly steamed vegetables. Good nutrition is not about forcing down unpalatable food, rather finding ways to increase your intake of nutrient dense ingredients in ways that you enjoy.

NUTRITIONAL VALUES PER SERVING: 274 calories, 26.5g total fat, 6.6mg cholesterol, 128.1mg sodium, 339.5mg potassium, 9.7g carbohydrates, 3.8g fibre, 1.7g sugar, 5.6g protein.

Light Tomato Sauce

This sauce, made with roasted cherry tomatoes, is a fresh lighter version than the rich glossy sauce made with tinned tomatoes. One of the best sources of antioxidants, tomatoes rid the body of damaging free radicals which are the cause of many modern diseases and degenerative aging. These compounds are more readily available when cooked and absorbed more readily when served with oil. Use this sauce as a simple coating for pasta, or as a base for other sauces. Don't just keep it for pasta, it can be used to dress meats, vegetables or as the basis of soups and stews. It will keep in the fridge for a week in an airtight container.

SERVINGS: 2
PREPARATION TIME: 10 minutes
COOKING TIME: 10 minutes

INGREDIENTS

2 tbsp. olive oil
500 g cherry tomatoes
1 clove garlic
2 pinches sea salt
2 tbsp. fresh breadcrumbs
4 tbsp. parsley
Plenty freshly ground
　　black pepper

1. Heat half of the oil in a frying pan and add the tomatoes with the whole garlic clove.

2. Cook over a high heat, shaking the pan occasionally, for about 10 minutes or until the tomatoes have softened and charred slightly around the outside.

3. Add salt and pepper and set aside to cool; just for 5 or 10 minutes.

4. Place the tomatoes with the remaining olive oil, parsley, salt, pepper and breadcrumbs into the large cup. Blend until you reach the desired consistency.

5. Return to the pan to heat and serve hot with a spoonful of crème fraiche if you want a creamy version.

NUTRITIONAL VALUES PER SERVING: 200 calories, 14.6g total fat, 0mg cholesterol, 356.8mg sodium, 572.2mg potassium, 16.5g carbohydrates, 3.1g fibre, <1g sugar, 3.1g protein.

Parsley and Parmesan Oil

Herb oils are a quick and impressive way to garnish all sorts of dishes from soups to elaborate main courses. Usually, the main ingredients would be discarded with just the flavoured oil remaining; the benefit being a longer shelf life but the down side of throwing away vital nutrients. As something to use immediately, or within a few days, leaving the bits in is fine. Don't be alarmed when it solidifies in the fridge; it will soon melt at room temperature. Packed full of herbs, this is a good way to maximise nutrients in a small space. Use to toss a plate of cooked pasta for a simple yet elegant meal. Once you get the hang of it, you can play about with all sorts of flavours; the key here though is that this is an oil. You don't want a thick sludge of herbs that loses the fine coating capacity of oil.

SERVINGS: 4

PREPARATION TIME: 15 minutes

INGREDIENTS

100 ml olive oil

50 g parsley, roughly chopped

1 tbsp. Parmesan, grated

1 lemon, zest only

1. Pulse all of the ingredients together in the large cup.

2. Store in a screw top container in the fridge, for up to 3 days, and bring to room temperature before serving.

NUTRITIONAL VALUES PER SERVING: 212 calories, 23.3g total fat, 1.1mg cholesterol, 26.7mg sodium, 73.4mg potassium, 1.1g carbohydrates, <1g fibre, <1g sugar, <1g protein.

Pepper, Tomato, and Olive Sauce

You could use the rich tomato sauce, or the light tomato sauce, for this recipe as well as making use of ready-made roasted peppers. Peppers and tomatoes are a classic combination that delivers not only on flavour but a double dose of those antioxidant lycopenes. Use the sauce as a coating for pasta or a springboard for other ingredients. You could layer cooked vegetables in a baking dish, drape with the sauce and top with cheese. Bake in the oven until bubbling for a quick veggie bake.

SERVINGS: 2
PREPARATION TIME: 10 minutes

INGREDIENTS

½ recipe light tomato sauce
100 g roasted red peppers
50 g Kalamata olives, pitted
2 tbsp. parsley

1. Pulse all of the ingredients together in the large cup to form a chunky sauce; pepper and olives should still be visible.

2. Reheat to use immediately or keep in the fridge for up to 5 days.

NUTRITIONAL VALUES PER SERVING: 131 calories, 10.4g total fat, 0mg cholesterol, 489.5mg sodium, 252.6mg potassium, 9.2g carbohydrates, 2g fibre, <1g sugar, 1.3g protein.

Rich Tomato Sauce

This slow cooked thick glossy version of tomato sauce is made with tinned tomatoes. The longer you cook it, the better it gets. You can make a passable sauce in 30 minutes by using plenty of tomato puree and turning the heat right up. If you have several hours to spare and some lovely fragrant fresh herbs then it really is worth taking the scenic route. Despite the slow cook, it could not actually be easier to make. This thick sauce will cling gloriously to pasta, drape lovingly over chicken breasts and make an excellent aubergine parmigiana.

SERVINGS: 4
PREPARATION TIME: 10 minutes
COOKING TIME: 1 hour

INGREDIENTS

1 bulb garlic
1 tin chopped tomatoes
2 tbsp. tomato puree
1 sprig fresh thyme
1 sprig fresh rosemary
1 bay leaf
1 sprig fresh thyme
½ tsp sea salt
2 tbsp. olive oil

1. Cut the garlic bulb in half, horizontally across the centre.
2. Put all of the ingredients into a large saucepan and set over a low heat. If you are taking the quick route, fill the empty can with a quarter water and pour in. Stir in the tomato puree.
3. If you are taking the slow route then add a full can of water.
4. Leave the whole lot to cook, with as much time as you have, stirring occasionally. The quick version will thicken but the long version will become thick and glossy. Craters will form on the surface that show you have a really good slow cooked sauce.
5. Leave the sauce to cool and pulse in the large cup to your desired thickness when ready.

NUTRITIONAL VALUES PER SERVING: 87 calories, 6.9g total fat, 0mg cholesterol, 369.2mg sodium, 207.9mg potassium, 6.1g carbohydrates, 1.1g fibre, 2.2g sugar, 1.2g protein.

Rocket, Tomato, and Onion Sauce

Rocket is a great way to get green nutrients and is often the salad leaf de jour. It can also be cooked just like spinach, leaving you with more options than just salad. As well as high levels of vitamin C and A, both antioxidant vitamins, rocket contains anti-cancer compounds that stimulate detoxifying enzymes in the blood. With a healthy dose of essential minerals too, rocket deserves a more prominent place on the dinner table; especially for those who shy away from spinach. Here, we use one of our tomato sauce bases, and add it to wilted rocket and cooked onion for a nutritious and delicious sauce. Use it to bring life to pasta or add to sausage and potato hash for a comforting meal.

SERVINGS: 2
PREPARATION TIME: 10 minutes
COOKING TIME: 10 minutes

INGREDIENTS

1 tbsp. olive oil
1 onion, thickly sliced
50 g rocket
Freshly ground black pepper
½ recipe rich tomato sauce

1. Heat the olive oil in a frying pan and add the onions. Cook for roughly 10 minutes over a medium slow heat until they are soft and browned.

2. Add the rocket to the frying pan for just as long as it takes to start wilting. Remove from the heat and season with plenty of freshly ground black pepper.

3. Place all of the ingredients in the large cup and pulse with the extractor blade for just long enough to combine.

4. Reheat the sauce to serve.

NUTRITIONAL VALUES PER SERVING: 113 calories, 8.7g total fat, 0mg cholesterol, 101.7mg sodium, 238.9mg potassium, 8.4g carbohydrates, 1.8g fibre, 3.7g sugar, 1.7g protein.

Salsa Verde

A cold sauce, traditionally served with meat or fish, we see no reason why salsa verde cannot be tossed with pasta or used as a general condiment. As well as the ubiquitous health promoting garlic, this sauce contains a fair amount of beneficial herbs and all their relevant greenness. Mint, a well-known digestive, has anti-cancer properties and is said to work in the prevention of allergies. Basil, also good for the digestion, is classically used to cure headaches and relieve sinuses; it also has anti-cancer compounds. Parsley, is also full of vitamin C and iron. This is a sharp, tangy sauce, which will liven up the taste buds and any dish you choose to pair it with. Try it with your morning eggs for a zingy wake up call.

SERVINGS: 4
PREPARATION TIME: 15 minutes

INGREDIENTS

½ clove garlic
½ red onion
2 anchovies
1 tbsp. capers
1 tbsp. Dijon mustard
1 tbsp. white wine vinegar
20 g parsley
20 g basil
20 g mint
4 tbsp. olive oil
1 pinch sea salt
Freshly ground black pepper

1. Pulse all of the ingredients together in the large cup to form a sauce.

2. Serve cold; it will keep in the fridge for a few days.

NUTRITIONAL VALUES PER SERVING: 138 calories, 13.9g total fat, 1.7mg cholesterol, 224.4mg sodium, 92.3mg potassium, 3g carbohydrates, 1.1g fibre, <1g sugar, 1.4g protein.

Sauce Vierge

A French oil-based sauce, sauce vierge is a light, fresh tasting addition to simply grilled fish or chicken but is quite as happy as a dressing, or even a sauce for pasta; to keep the sauce cold rather than hot try using it to dress a cold pasta salad.

SERVINGS: 4

PREPARATION TIME: 15 minutes

INGREDIENTS

100 g cherry tomatoes
2 tsp capers
½ lemon, juice and zest
½ red onion, chopped
100 ml olive oil
30 g chives
1 tbsp. coriander seeds
Freshly ground black pepper

1. Pulse all of the ingredients together in the large cup to form a chunky sauce; it should be chunky with bits of ingredients suspended in oil.

2. Serve cold; it is best used all at once.

NUTRITIONAL VALUES PER SERVING: 222 calories, 23.3g total fat, 0mg cholesterol, 43.5mg sodium, 107.3mg potassium, 4.5g carbohydrates, 1.3g fibre, <1g sugar, <1g protein.

Spicy Aubergine and Coconut Sauce

A sort of quick half curry, half sauce to be served over rice, this recipe makes use of the aubergine's ability to take on other flavours and pairs them with the versatility of coconut milk. You could add any number of vegetables to the mix to boost the nutrient content, or add them in to the rice pilau style. You could of course just serve it as is and enjoy a simple comforting meal.

SERVINGS: 2
PREPARATION TIME: 10 minutes
COOKING TIME: 20 minutes

INGREDIENTS

1 aubergine, diced
1 onion, sliced
1 tbsp. coconut oil
1 red chilli, chopped
25 mm ginger, grated
1 clove garlic
1 tsp coriander seed
1 tsp nutmeg
½ tsp turmeric
100 ml coconut milk
1 pinch sea salt
Freshly ground black pepper
2 tbsp. fresh coriander
2 tbsp. fresh mint

TO GARNISH

Coriander
Mint
Fresh lime

1. Heat the coconut oil in a frying pan and add the aubergine with a pinch of salt.

2. Fry the aubergine until brown on the outside and soft in the middle. Once ready, set aside.

3. Put the rest of the ingredients into the large cup and add one third of the cooked aubergine. Pulse until almost smooth; what you are looking for is a smooth yet thick sauce with flecks of herbs and chilli. Add more coconut milk if too thick.

4. Return the frying pan with the aubergine to the heat and pour in the spiced coconut sauce. Heat to serve and garnish with more fresh herbs and a squeeze of lime juice.

NUTRITIONAL VALUES PER SERVING: 271 calories, 18.6g total fat, 0mg cholesterol, 160.6mg sodium, 891.8mg potassium, 27.4g carbohydrates, 9.4g fibre, 12.4g sugar, 4.7g protein.

Squash and Sage

Orange winter type squash such as butternut and pumpkin are full of beneficial carotenes and have a positive effect on blood sugar levels. Sage and butternut is a classic combination, and the soft squash is perfectly suited for pairing with pasta as a comforting yet nutritious meal.

SERVINGS: 2
PREPARATION TIME: 10 minutes
COOKING TIME: 20 minutes

INGREDIENTS

1 small butternut squash
1 onion, chopped
½ clove garlic
4 sage leaves
1 pinch salt
Freshly ground black pepper
1 squeeze lemon juice
100 ml chicken stock

1. Place all of the ingredients in a large pan, cover, and bring gently to a boil. Turn the heat down low and simmer gently for about 15 minutes or until the squash is soft.

2. Remove the garlic and the sage leaves; this time we want just a subtle hint of flavour, not the full force.

3. Leave the contents of the pan to cool and then transfer to the large cup. Pulse just a little, to mix the ingredients to create a sauce, but not overly smooth.

4. Reheat to serve; with chunky pasta or even rice.

NUTRITIONAL VALUES PER SERVING: 90 calories, <1g total fat, 1.5mg cholesterol, 223.5mg sodium, 505.8mg potassium, 19.9g carbohydrates, 3.2g fibre, 5.7g sugar, 3g protein.

Wild Mushroom Sauce

Most wild varieties of mushrooms differ greatly, nutritionally speaking, from the cultivated white mushrooms that we so easily reach for. Generally speaking they are a good source of iron and selenium, as well as exhibiting benefits such as anti-cancer activity and strengthening of immune function. Not only that, but wild type mushrooms are full of intense incredible flavour and have a texture often compared to meat. The best ways with such mushrooms are the simple ones, so a quick sauté in butter and a generous seasoning of salt and pepper is all they need to perform at their best. Beyond that, a few flecks of parsley and a dash of something creamy is as far as you need go. Use this sauce to dress pasta, or to adorn chicken and meat. Chicken stock rounds out the flavours well but use water if you do not have.

SERVINGS: 2
PREPARATION TIME: 10 minutes
COOKING TIME: 10 minutes

INGREDIENTS

200 g fresh wild mushrooms, mixed
2 tbsp. butter
1 pinch sea salt
Freshly ground black pepper
2 tbsp. parsley
2 tbsp. fresh white breadcrumbs
50 ml chicken stock
2 tbsp. crème fraiche

1. Heat the butter in a large frying pan and add the mushrooms with plenty of seasoning.

2. Cook over a medium high heat, for about 3 minutes, shaking the pan every now and then. Remove from the heat.

4. Add one third of the mushrooms to the small cup with the rest of the ingredients and pulse until smooth.

5. Pour the resulting sauce back into the pan, stir through the mushrooms and reheat to serve.

NUTRITIONAL VALUES PER SERVING: 439 calories, 15.2g total fat, 37.5mg cholesterol, 216.7mg sodium, 1604.8mg potassium, 78.1g carbohydrates, 11.7g fibre, <1g sugar, 10.8g protein.

DIPS AND DRESSINGS

How about a few healthy and flavoursome dressings to complete this selection of ideas for getting the most from your NutriBullet. Sometimes we like to graze and munch our way through a film, or provide a healthy snack for guests or children, and not everything has to be laden with mayonnaise or full of sugar. Serve healthy dips with crudités, breadsticks or even the occasional handful of root crisps and experiment with different flavours to dress your salads and vegetable dishes.

Artichoke, Lemon, and Garlic Dip

Artichokes are a great source of dietary fibre, and provide many essential minerals. They also contain inulin, a compound shown to improve blood sugar control. Difficult to find raw, choose tinned artichokes instead. Lemons are not only a good source of vitamin C, but consuming lemon juice at the beginning of a meal is said to slow down the effects of food on blood sugars. Garlic of course has many magical properties; fighting infection and cancer to name just a few.

SERVINGS: 2
PREPARATION TIME: 15 minutes

INGREDIENTS

100 g artichoke hearts
½ lemon, juice only
1 pinch salt
2 cloves garlic
1 tbsp. olive oil

Pulse everything in the small cup with the milling blade until the desired consistency is achieved. Serve straight away so it does not discolour.

NUTRITIONAL VALUES PER SERVING: 96 calories, 6.9g total fat, 0mg cholesterol, 193.8mg sodium, 219.6mg potassium, 8.6g carbohydrates, 2.9g fibre, <1g sugar, 2g protein.

Avocado Dressing

Green goddess dressing has been around for a while and is the perfect beauty booster for clear skin. Full of the many benefits of the healthful fatty acids it contains, this wonderful food does not deserved to be shunned for its calorie content. The smooth silky texture translates beautifully into a dressing and acts as a vehicle for plenty of green herbs too.

SERVINGS: 4
PREPARATION TIME: 15 minutes

INGREDIENTS

1 small ripe avocado
1 tbsp. olive oil
1 clove garlic
1 pinch salt
1 tbsp. lemon juice
4 tbsp. parsley
100 ml water

Pulse everything in the small cup with the milling blade until the desired consistency is achieved. Serve straight away so it does not discolour.

NUTRITIONAL VALUES PER SERVING: 105 calories, 10.1g total fat, 0mg cholesterol, 79.2mg sodium, 247.6mg potassium, 4.5g carbohydrates, 3.1g fibre, <1g sugar, 1g protein.

Caper Vinaigrette

A rounded yet sharp vinaigrette with the added tang of capers. Keep in a recycled bottle or jar in the fridge for up to 5 days. You could use this dressing as a base for any number of other ideas to pep up your salads or even hot vegetable sides; add green herbs, olives, raspberries or mango. You may wish to omit the capers if you add sweet elements though! You can use any oil, or source of acidity that pleases you.

SERVINGS: 4
PREPARATION TIME: 15 minutes

INGREDIENTS

8 tbsp. olive oil
2 tbsp. white wine vinegar
1 pinch salt
1 tsp mustard
2 tbsp. capers

Pulse everything in the small cup with the milling blade. Enjoy!

NUTRITIONAL VALUES PER SERVING: 242 calories, 27.1g total fat, 0mg cholesterol, 206.5mg sodium, 11.2mg potassium, <1g carbohydrates, <1g fibre, <1g sugar, <1g protein.

Roasted Pepper and Balsamic Dressing

You could use pre roasted red peppers for this recipe or roast your own. If you roast your own, it is worth doing a batch and keeping them in the fridge for up to 5 days; it is nice to roast the garlic too so do some alongside. Peppers are one of the most nutrient dense foods around and deliver an array of health benefits. Lycopene, for heart protection, is present in peppers as well as tomatoes and they are also an excellent source of vitamin C.

SERVINGS: 4
PREPARATION TIME: 15 minutes

INGREDIENTS

50 g roasted red peppers
8 tbsp. olive oil
2 tbsp. balsamic vinegar
2 tbsp. parsley
1 pinch sea salt

Pulse everything in the small cup with the milling blade until the desired consistency is achieved.

NUTRITIONAL VALUES PER SERVING: 250 calories, 27g total fat, 0mg cholesterol, 74.2mg sodium, 41.9mg potassium, 2.3g carbohydrates, <1g fibre, 1.2g sugar, <1g protein.

Smoky Mango Salsa

You will need chipotle chillies to get the smoky aspect of this fruity salsa. Chipotle are smoked and dried jalapeno peppers; readily available in dried or powder form nowadays they are a wonderful way to get smoky heat into your food. They are reasonably hot though. If you use dried chipotle, reconstitute them in hot water and use as you would fresh chilli; otherwise just use as chilli powder. We would recommend seeking out the whole dried ones for the best results and they will come in handy for so many dishes.

SERVINGS: 2
PREPARATION TIME: 15 minutes

INGREDIENTS

1 large ripe mango,
    flesh only
1 red onion, chopped
½ clove garlic, crushed
1 tsp paprika
1 lime, juice only
2 tbsp. coriander, chopped
1 tsp chipotle chilli
    (more if required)
1 pinch sea salt

Pulse everything in the small cup with the milling blade until the desired consistency is achieved. Serve straight away so it does not discolour.

NUTRITIONAL VALUES PER SERVING: 145 calories, 1.3g total fat, 0mg cholesterol, 177.2mg sodium, 476.2mg potassium, 35.7g carbohydrates, 6.1g fibre, 23.9g sugar, 3.1g protein.

Spinach and Bean Dip

A creamy bean dip for sharing a crudité platter with friends or a healthy yet solitary snack in front of the TV. Although the beans are a good source of protein and offer many health benefits besides, here they are simply a vehicle for the spinach. Far more nutritious than mayonnaise and with a more robust texture, beans are the best way to go when something creamy is required. Spinach is known for its iron content but is also full of anti-cancerous compounds, vitamin c and helps prevent against macular degeneration; something we tend not to consider when thinking about health in old age.

SERVINGS: 4
PREPARATION TIME: 15 minutes

INGREDIENTS

50 g spinach
1 tin butter beans
2 tbsp. olive oil
1 pinch salt
1 clove garlic
½ lemon, juice only
2 tbsp. fresh mint or parsley

Place all of the ingredients in the large cup and pulse with the extractor blade until the desired consistency is reached. The dip is great when left chunky but if you want something smoother then you may need a drop or two of water.

NUTRITIONAL VALUES PER SERVING: 156 calories, 7.2g total fat, 0mg cholesterol, 362.2mg sodium, 376mg potassium, 18g carbohydrates, 6.2g fibre, 2.5g sugar, 6.2g protein.

CONCLUSION

And that's a wrap, folks! The power of the NutriBullet can be used to create much more than tasty and delicious smoothies, all while harnessing the pure goodness of fruits and vegetables that is often lost through more conventional methods of preparation. By focusing on flavour and using the best combinations of raw and cooked produce, your NutriBullet can become just another part of your daily kitchen arsenal to make nutritious and delicious meals that you can enjoy every single day of the week.

I hope that you love these recipes as much as I do and that they soon replace unhealthier options in your kitchen. Cheers to a full belly and your great health!

Until next time—ciao!

Diana Clayton

Recommendations for More Low-Calorie Goodness

Hungry for more? Pick up the latest editions of low-calorie books from Diana. Just search Amazon for "Diana Clayton" and discover even more incredible recipes, all while shedding some pounds. Diana's low calorie cookbook collection includes ...

81 Super Healthy & Fat Burning NutriBullet Smoothie Recipes to Lose Weight and Enhance Health

Healthy & Nutritious Smoothie Recipes for Weight Loss, Improved Health, and Happiness

Heavenly Slow Cooker Recipes from All Around the World, All Under 500 Calories!

Healthy & Filling 5:2 Fast Diet Recipes to Lose Weight and Enhance your Health

Amazing Single Serving 5:2 Fast Diet Recipes to Lose More Weight with Intermittent Fasting

14624552R00057

Printed in Great Britain
by Amazon.co.uk, Ltd.,
Marston Gate.